T0082542

Life in the Navy Reserves

by Cameron Douglas McPherson

Trafford rev. 06/27/2023

 www.trafford.com

North America & international
toll-free: 844-688-6899 (USA & Canada)
fax: 812 355 4082

TABLE OF CONTENTS

ACKNOWLEDGMENTS

I would like to thank my mother Inge Hendricks for whom my career would not have lasted as long as it did had she not prevented me from quitting after just two years of service. To my grandfather Norm McPherson who also served in the Navy, and was a great source of inspiration for me as I went through the same boot camp he did during my basic training. And to the many sailors, men and women, who helped me to form such cherished memories. I am proud to call them all friends. I would like to mention just a few: LS Jason van Reyen, LS Jeremy Nixon C.D., LS Leo Castillo, LS Trevor Schaffrick, LS Patrick Boulanger, MS Keith Brown C.D., and LS (retired) Rick Bennett C.D. I looked up to Rick during my career, before he retired; he had the longest active career in our mess at the time.

Many thanks to LT. (Navy) Ian Bernard at HMCS Nonsuch for his involvement on this project. He graciously accepted my offer to be the first person to read this book in its entirety. My meeting with Ian was the last roadblock on my way to publishing, and when I met with him, he was very positive about the book. For that, I am thankful.

I wish to extend a thank you to my work partner in my civilian job, Cory Urbanovitch. I spent a lot of time at work telling Cory of my adventures, and he always had an ear to lend. I consider myself fortunate to have had the opportunity to work with, and learn from such a talented tradesman.

I thank my brother Darren McPherson, who always helped me find civilian employment through his connections. He has been such an asset to my family, and I attribute much of my success to him. Darren also lent his skills to this project, as he helped with formatting and editing. Thanks as well to Dawn Edwards my other editor. Dawn's input was very much appreciated, and well respected.

A heartfelt thank you as well to my sister Trisha Pangrass, and her husband Wayne for providing me with a place to stay in the city while I attended training nights with the Reserves.

Thanks to a long time friend Rob Fenske, who was best man at my wedding. I've known Rob for quite some time now, and he's been a good friend to count on throughout the years.

I reserve a very special thank you to my ever-loving wife Kellie McPherson for her constant support of my endeavors. She always let me know that it was all right when I had to leave home for duty. And she also encouraged me to do my best, and to stay active in the Forces longer than I thought I could. Also to my children Keegon, and Shayna, thank you as well for your support.

Finally, I would like to dedicate this book to the memory of my father, Doug McPherson. In passing, he taught me the value of life. Thank you dad.

BOOT CAMP

One day in the late fall of 1991 while I was sitting in a Social Studies class at my High School, a couple of recruiters came in to talk to our class about joining the Navy Reserves the following summer. For the most part the other students weren't interested, and I'm not terribly sure that I was either, but for some reason I took their literature home to show my parents. It was a surprise that I even made it home without losing the papers. I wasn't much of a student in high school, and my life didn't seem to be going in any direction. My parents were aware of this, and I wanted to show them that I wasn't the lazy sleepy eyed teenager they thought I was.

My stepfather had spent some time in the militia, and he told me how proud he was of my decision, but he didn't want me to do it just to impress him. He told me that military life was going to be a tough go for me, and that I would have to be quite prepared mentally as well as physically for the demanding challenges that were ahead of me.

I knew I had something to prove, even though I wasn't sure myself if I was capable of completing the task. But I thought once I got there I would do my best to take it one step at a time, and never give up. There's a certain amount of maturity required to get through an ordeal like that. And looking back, it's hard to believe that I was able to do what I did at seventeen. But in the end, that notch on my belt turned me into a man. The confidence and satisfaction of what I did will remain with me for the rest of my life.

Sitting with my C7 rifle

For the rest of the winter and on into spring, I went though all the required stages to sign up for the military, and on May 04 1992, I was sworn in. For the next two months, I trained at my home unit with a group of eager young men and women, waiting to do their country proud.

Then, all too soon it was the eve of my trip, and I'll never forget the last supper I had with my parents. I knew they were proud of me that day. They took me out to the place of my choice; it felt like it was my birthday. That night it was difficult for me to sleep, the most challenging time of my life was about to begin.

Morning came, July 09 1992, for me "A day that will live in infamy." As I made my way to the airport with my parents, my sister lay in the hospital waiting to give birth to her first two children. I was going to be an uncle for the first time that day. But visiting them would have to wait for a couple of months. This definitely lent to my sadness over having to leave my family. And when the time came to say goodbye at the airport, speaking as a young man who had never been away from home on his own, it was one of the most gut wrenching moments of my life.

Nonetheless I boarded the plane to make the long journey to the other end of this great country of ours. There were a few stops along the way, at each one we would pick up more recruits. When our plane touched down for the final time in Nova Scotia it was already dark outside, it had been a long day. As I waited for my luggage, I set my watch ahead three hours.

Once everyone rounded up their luggage, we were directed onto a bus. On the bus, the mood was somber, and everyone onboard was tired. I sat quietly and listened to the whispers of recruits getting acquainted as we bumped along through the darkness. But once we arrived at the base it became all too real that the road ahead of us was going to get a whole lot bumpier.

From the moment the bus doors opened, and for the next 51 days, the yelling started. "Come on, come on, you worthless bags of shit, get off that fuckin' bus and fall in line. Let's go, let's go, let's go, this isn't fucking summer vacation."   They would occasionally stop and draw attention to some poor guy, but they let us all know in short order that we were all worthless.

View of the barracks

The rules were simple; we trained in the day, and believe me we trained hard. And at night we would put on our coveralls that were labeled with our serial number and work on our uniforms, or study. There was no time for leisure, and we were confined to barracks like prisoners. There was no place to sit inside the barracks. You had to sit on the floor, but you had better have your hands busy or you might find yourself doing more pushups than you can handle while your buddies watched. Sitting on your bed before "lights out" was a chargeable offense, and you did not want to suffer those consequences.

All of our civilian items were taken from us and locked away. We were taken down to the base barber to have our heads shaved, for which we had to pay five dollars. There was a diagram available on how we were to arrange our uniforms in our locker. No one person was to be different from another. The shelves in the locker were 25 inches wide. We had to iron our uniform shirts and fold them into 12 x 18-inch rectangles that were no more than 1 inch high each. The shirts sat in two piles of two, and there had to be exactly 1 inch between the two piles. You had to press your underwear and have it folded 4 x 4 inches exactly, and your instructor had to be able to see his reflection in your boots. It was very tedious to make your beds to the required standards, so you tried to only make it once. Everybody mostly slept on top of their beds wearing the coveralls to keep warm because it was mandatory that the windows remained open. Colds and flu's were rampant amongst us all.

The weekdays were filled with grueling exercise classes that made the older guys (mid to late 20's), look ancient. Seeing someone throw up their last meal was not uncommon, it was even less uncommon to see those same people getting yelled at for wasting the Queen's food in such a manner. We ran with rifles and gear in the hot sun, we climbed ropes, practiced carrying each other across the gym, worked with medicine balls, etc. Part of the day was spent in a classroom, but it was equally as challenging to try to stay awake never mind absorb what was being taught.

Boot polishing session

On the weekend, there was no time to catch up on anything you were behind in because those were the days we had to clean the building. Part of this job included stripping and waxing the floor with your bath towels on hands and knees. And if you didn't pull your weight here, you would be dealing with the rest of the guys in your squad. I watched more than a couple fights break out for these reasons. But I think a lot of fighting occurred due to pressure, frustrations, and other emotional breakdowns. It was a hard time; we all put in some hard time. The picture on the back of this book shows that. I look as though I just came back from a POW camp.

I came home that summer from a place where it was a necessity of life to find friendships and lean on each other through thick and thin. I could not have made it through that ordeal without some of the bonds that I formed. We were taught to be as one. If one of us fell, we all stopped to help. We were a strong unit, with a just cause: to "Stand on Guard for Thee."

Another thing that I learned from that summer is that I'm now a very fast eater, my wife will attest to that. But I've learned never to waste food, and always clear my plate.

FIRE FIGHTING IN HALIFAX

After graduating from basic training in 1992, a lot of the guys from boot camp went straight to their first trades course and most of them received promotion to Able Seaman in their first year of service. As for myself, promotion would have to wait because I had two more years of High School left to complete. But during those years, I spent as much time as I could honing my skills as a professional sailor by completing whatever tasks the Navy would allow me to do. Even though I was an Ordinary Seaman with no trade training, I was learning the trade through my own curiosity, and my own willingness to get involved in whatever training I was allowed to participate in. In addition I attended, and received certification for various safety standards required of me.

In my own view I was every bit as good as the Able Seamen I served with, and a lot of them thought of me as an Able Seaman. But my lack of career progression on paper was a strike against me that almost cost me my career in the Navy. By the time I was sent on my trade course I was the senior Ordinary Seaman of my unit and I had seen recruits who joined after me, receive their promotions ahead of me.

The graduation date for this course was November 04 1994. This coincided with my 2½-year anniversary in the reserves. This was significant because if you have not completed your first trades course after 2½ years of service you were liable for discharge. When notice came to take the course, I was given the choice to decline the offer, but that would have most certainly put an end to my career.

So on September 18, of 1994 I made my journey across the country for the second time in my career. My destination was Halifax, Nova Scotia, where I would spend the next 51 days learning the tricks of my trade, and paving the way for my first promotion. The skills I had developed prior to taking the course enabled me to breeze right through it, and I finished in third place. There were only two people who finished ahead of me, but they both had more experience. One guy came from a previous career in the regular forces, and there was a girl who had spent a few years as a cadet before joining the reserves. After completing the course, I would end up waiting until April of 1995 to be promoted, just one month shy of 3 years as an Ordinary Seaman.

I very much enjoyed my time in Halifax that year and to this day I still pass on the skills I learned there through my lectures and presentations here at home. But one of the things I learned out there that I can't teach my subordinates in a practical application was fire fighting. I have done a lot of fire fighting over the years in Victoria, BC, but this was my first kick at the can and I will always remember that one.

Flood training facility

The first day of the course was spent doing administration, and getting your bearings.   We did a lecture on sea survival, and a practical application in the pool. At day's end, we were told that in the morning there would be a bus to pick us up outside the barracks. We would be taken to Damage Control School for the next two weeks to train in fire fighting, flood control, and nuclear, biological and chemical warfare, for three days each.

Each course had a couple days of classroom time, and then one day of practical training inside mock compartments of vessels that contained fires, floods, or tear gas. In class we watched videos, and documentaries. We listened to lectures, and wrote tests. Then it was time for the real thing. We were escorted over to the firehouse to be issued our fire suits. I can remember the rush of adrenaline hitting me as I changed into my gear. I was hoping to stay in the change room as long as I could but the call to hurry up came quickly. We all came out of the change room, and formed up outside for a demonstration on how to properly wear the breathing devices. Then we partnered up to put them on each other.

The breathing devices we wore are called a Chemox, and they are strapped to the front of your body. They are made of a flexible rubber that expands and contracts like lungs. In the center, there is a compartment that accepts a cartridge. When fully in place inside the Chemox, the cartridge cover becomes punctured by a tube leading into the hoses that attach to your facemask. Once in place inside the Chemox, a pull-tab on a string will drop down from the cartridge. When you pull this tab out, a candle is lit producing oxygen. The cartridges are good for an hour, and when you look down at your Chemox while it is strapped to your chest, you will see a timer. For safety reasons the timers are set to 45 minutes to give you some time to get out of the fire.

We did a few team scenarios, were we burst into a compartment   from   the   main   door.   Inside   the compartment, there were two big engines in the middle of the room. We walked onto a floor made of grading that surrounded the engines. The fire raged from underneath the grading from a large pool of flammable liquid that was a few inches deep. It was very difficult to see anything through the smoke, so we were very careful not to trip, or become separated from the hose. It is extremely dangerous to become separated from the source of water, and because of the poor visibility, you can become lost in an instant. Even the fire itself is hard to see. Between billowing clouds of thick heavy grey and black smoke you see only the occasional rolling flicker of orange. But even that becomes distorted and blurry through the water droplets of condensation forming on your mask, and you seem to have no depth perception.

When you share a room with a fire out of control, I compare it to going into an unlit room and trying to find a set of keys, but a lot more hair raising. You have to feel your way through the room, forget about using your vision.   Here you must use your instincts, and there's nothing like a piece of flame darting out from behind a curtain of smoke and licking you on the mask to heighten them. Occasionally you bump into things as you do in the dark, and it is a luxury when you really know the layout of the room.

On the outside of the compartment, once the fire is lit inside it sounds like a raging monster. And the sounds inside are foreboding and ominous. But once inside, your mind takes over and you go into such a state of concentration that you seem to only hear your own breath, the wrinkling of your clothes, and the pounding of your heart. Voices and screams are muffled and incoherent, and the wide-eyed ferocity with which you attack the fire seems out of body.

View of the fire compartment

After fighting the engine room fire in groups of four, it was time to practice individual attacks. We climbed on top of a vessel simulating being on the upper decks. And one by one, we were supposed to descend into the vessel through a hatch on the deck, and then put out the fire. When my turn was up, I remembered a couple of things from my training. One was that you were never to let go of the hose; the hose was your life. The ladder was equipped with a handrail so you had to keep one hand on it at all times. The second thing I learned was that you do not put any external pressure on your Chemox. If you do, you run the risk of collapsing the lungs, and you need to be out in the fresh air to be able to revive them.

When I descended the ladder, I was clutching the hose nozzle so tightly against my chest that I forgot about the second rule. I went down the ladder quite quickly because it felt as though the adrenaline was making my knees week. At the bottom, I found that I had deflated my Chemox lungs. The mask clung to my face tighter and tighter when I breathed in, and when I breathed out the mask would lift slightly allowing air to escape out the sides. I wasn't getting any air and I was starting to suffocate. I tried to turn toward the ladder to go back up but suddenly I was grabbed and being held back. It was the instructor who lit the fire and I guess he was yelling at me to put it out. I couldn't see him that well and I tried yelling back at him that my lungs had collapsed, but we couldn't hear each other. At this point I was trying to pull the mask off my face to breathe whatever air I could. I started choking as I breathed in the smoke, and for a second time I tried to go up the ladder. The instructor held me back again; he didn't want me going anywhere because I had the water.

So I just said screw it, I let go of my mask, held my breath, and took aim at the fire. With the hatch above me open, I had some limited vision, and to me the fire looked like a flickering candle off in the distance. Actually it was a large trunk filled with flammable liquid. When my water hit the trunk the liquid inside splashed out violently and that little flickering flame erupted and roared towards me like an angry beast. Time seemed to stand still at that moment as I watched in awe as these huge flames came toward me tumbling faster and faster, and growing larger and larger. It really only took less than a second for the flames to hit me in the chest and knock me into the wall. Now it was my turn to erupt. I pulled on that hose valve as hard as I could making sure it was fully open as I began to advance on my enemy. I thrashed around and yelled at the fire until I had won the battle. It took only a few moments for the smoke to billow out of the hatch, and within seconds I could see again. I dropped my hose, pulled off my mask, and breathed a sigh of relief.

A NIGHT OUT IN DOWNTOWN VANCOUVER

In May of 2001, I traveled to Vancouver with a small group of sailors, all from Edmonton, to do a minor boating exercise. Our home unit had sent an advance party out to drive our R.H.I.B. (rigid hull inflatable boat), and we were going to borrow a second R.H.I.B. from the unit stationed near Stanley Park in Vancouver.

Our journey started out with a mid afternoon plane trip on a Friday. When we landed in Vancouver there was still a lot of daylight. Me and a couple of friends decided to catch a limo to the base, which sort of became a tradition for a small group of us every time we were out that way. Somehow the driver got our directions mixed up, so we went for a very scenic drive around some pretty nice and high-class neighborhoods. The weather was beautiful, and we rode around town with the stereo turned up and the windows rolled down.

When we arrived at the base, the commissioner met us at the gate to check us in. Then we went up the hill to our barracks. The base was a ghost town as the training year ends for most units after the first weekend in May. When we got into the barracks we noticed that the building was under renovations, and we all had to sleep in one big office on cots. Our advance party had signed out all the cots, but we had to assemble them ourselves.

After getting all settled in, it was time to pile into the company trucks and go downtown for supper. When we arrived in Gastown, we parked the trucks and decided to walk around looking for a good place to eat. We all decided on the Spaghetti Factory, and while were waiting in line outside the restaurant, our adventure began.

A crazy man pushing a shopping cart and screaming, came barreling towards us. When he reached us he was yelling that his cart was full of broken glass, and that we needed to give him money because he collected the glass for our safety. The guy looked like he was wearing make up, and he had the worst case of bed head I had ever seen. Because of this, one of our guys started to laugh at him. That's when the guy started to lose it. He told us not to laugh at him saying, "I wouldn't laugh if I were you, you don't know who I am, you don't know where I got these tattoos, you don't know where I got these bullet wounds!" He lifted his shirt to show some scars, but I didn't see any. He told us not to go much further down this street because it would be too dangerous for us. Then he started to reach into his cart for a shard of broken glass. That's when we decided to move along.

Aboard the RHIB with Pat & Leo

Not much more than half a minute later, we found ourselves being accosted by a man claiming to be schizophrenic and showing us a card. After that our group split up, and only four of us carried on down the street. We found a pizza joint, but just outside there was a guy wanting to sell us some drugs. We passed by him and went in to buy a slice of pizza each. There was nowhere to sit inside, so we had to go sit on the bench outside. I ended up sitting next to a guy wearing a suit. He looked like he had a sandwich in his hand but he wasn't eating it and when he first joined in on our conversation, he seemed pretty normal. But when one of our guys walked over to the trash to throw his crust out, the guy got up and said, "Don't do that". Then he walked over to the trash, fished out the crust, and started eating it.

Then he started talking about some wild pot party he went to last weekend. The guy looked middle-aged, and it was odd to hear him talk about a wild pot-party, but we just listened to him and laughed along with him. Then he gave us the same foreboding message about continuing on down the street.

We decided to get into our truck and drive down this street that everyone kept talking about. Sure enough, it looked like hell on earth. Some of the streetlights were out, there was graffiti everywhere, people were walking around smoking crack or carrying stolen items, and some people were just passed out on the ground.

We carried on from there to find a pub to spend the rest of the night at. But before going into the pub, a group of men told us they would guard our truck for a small fee because they were going to be in the parking lot all night. And just before going in to the bar, a drunk lady who could barely walk, asked us for some money. When we told her we didn't have any, she noticed one of our guys was drinking a juice, so she asked for the bottle.

At the end of the night when we got back to our truck, the men in the parking lot surrounded us and started to demand money. We all just jumped in the truck and drove of. What a place!

DECOMMISSIONING THE DE LA REINE

In December of 1996, I was sent out to Victoria BC, to help decommission a gate vessel. It was the last gate vessel on the West Coast to go. And out of all them, this was the one I had spent the most time on, and I was sad to see her go.

Back in September, my home unit HMCS Nonsuch, sent out a crew to sail on her for the last time. I did that trip with them, and I remember it being like a mini decommissioning trip. Afterwards, our ship's company posed in front of her for a final picture.

That December however, was the absolute last time the De La Reine would sail with any crew, her final run. The crew was made up of sailors from Edmonton, Calgary, and Saskatoon. During the flight to the coast, I read the schedule and there was supposed to be a big wind-up party afterwards in full rigs. I was excited, and deeply honored to be a part of the De La Reine's last trip.

My previous service on her contributed greatly to my promotion to leading seaman. She was an old friend, and I wouldn't have missed her send off.

I remember the night I crossed the brow onto the ship, and how I saluted her briskly. I had never sailed before in December, and there was a chill in the air. There was also a lot of adrenaline and memories buzzing around in my head. I rushed down the hatch and threw my bag on the rack I usually had, claiming it for the one-week trip. Then I went back up top to read the Watch and Station Bill.

Driving the De La Reine

There's a position on a ship called the special sea duty position, often referred to as "Specials". The ship goes into "Specials" when she enters or leaves harbor, goes through a narrow straight, or when she encounters hazardous or dangerous seas. This means in theory, that if any of these conditions exist, the best man will be manning each important position.

Up to this point, I was used to seeing my name on the manning pool list during "Specials". The manning pool is a way to collect all the sailors who don't have a special sea duty position, to task them off as necessary or to simply keep them out of the way. I was expecting to be on the manning pool again this time. I was probably the most junior Leading Seaman onboard, having been at the rank for only half a year, and I never had a special sea duty position before anyway. Mostly, I just wanted to know which watch I was on.

When I looked up my name, I stood there in shock. Under special sea duty and across from my name, it said helmsman. This meant that I would be the last sailor to take the helm when our ship came to her final rest. I remember thinking that this was some sort of mistake, and that there were other leading seamen onboard who were more qualified than me. I was completely honored, but also nervous as hell.

Sure I've driven the boat before, but never in and out of harbor when it takes all your concentration and skills. I didn't even know the procedure for reporting that I was on the helm. Another thing that was new to me was that there was a tape recorder to turn on before I delivered my turnover speech. It would record the whole time I was in "Specials", like a black box.

Next morning came and soon it was time to drive the ship out. The first thing I did when I came onto the bridge was to memorize my speech. I was nervous but composed, and in the end I did a wonderful job. Over the coarse of the trip, I started to realize the other benefits of being the SSD helmsmen. Whenever there was an upper deck evolution that required rigging in the cold, they needed me to drive to deliver a smooth ride. So I often got out of doing all the cold upper deck work.

I remember one night while I was training a girl to drive; we went into rough seas. All of a sudden the ship started to make a sharp turn, the girl didn't know what was happening and she tried to counter steer. She gave the helm a modest turn and it wasn't responding that well. At this point, I stood up and began to turn on the tape and give my speech, and then I took control of the helm. Most of the crew was asleep, and the officer on watch looked like he was going to get on the intercom and wake the ship. He asked me if I was OK, because he could see me violently working the helm back and forth. I was full of adrenaline so I just said yes, and kept working. Looking back on that moment, I guess I might have taken the life of the crew into my own hands.

To me the waves were like moguls on a ski hill, when the boat hit the wave on one side the ship would turn away like a car skidding out of control. I just kept turning into the skids until I thought I could do no more, luckily that was the point at which we got out of the rough patch. Feeling exhausted, I turned the helm back over to the girl, and I sat down to take a rest.

A ship sailing in formation with ours

The last day of the trip was exciting for me in a different way. I sailed the De La Reine home, sailing in formation with a couple other larger warships. There was supposed to be a party that night, and everyone was excited. I remember approaching the entrance to the harbor when people would come in to take a last crack at the helm. There were a lot of pictures being snapped off in there, it really was something else.

Then when we got close enough to the harbor, I took the helm and drove her in. It was a little hard to concentrate that day, there were a lot of people crammed in the bridge, and a lot of them were taking my picture as well. To me that day marks one of the most memorable

and enjoyable for me. Goodbye Miss De La Reine, you will
be missed.

MEETING THE PREMIER

The first annual Reserve Day parade was held in Edmonton, on June 6th of 1999. Every year thereafter, the parade is held in a different city. While most sailors in the Reserves take on full time contracts in the summer, I stayed at home with my pregnant wife Kellie. Needless to say, I was on hand for the parade and it was an honor to take part in it.

Before the actual day came, we had a couple of practice nights at my home unit. At these practices, we were issued with white gloves and belts for our black dress uniforms. This was my first "White Glove" parade. I've paraded for the Mayor before, but never for the Premier. Also, this was my first time with a fixed bayonet on my rifle. During the practices I would overhear horror stories about people getting injured from the bayonets. I heard one story about a guy who went to shoulder his weapon and slashed it open requiring several stitches. Another story told of how one person passed out from exhaustion, and on his way down, his bayonet made a deep cut on the back of the person in front of him. Whether or not these stories were true, they put me on edge and gave me more respect for my rifle.

On Parade at the Legislature grounds

At practise it was decided that I would be the right marker in the front rank for our division. This meant that once we arrived on parade and the order "Right dress", was given, I was responsible for moving into the correct position first and the rest of the division would line up on my mark. I was happy to be given such a distinctive position in the parade because I knew my wife and parents were going to be in the audience taking pictures, and this way I could tell them where to find me.

Before the actual parade started, as our division was waiting at the legislature grounds, I was given some last words of advice. I was told that we would be marched onto paraded, halted, and then turned forward to face the legislature building. At this point, the parade commander would take over and I might have to shuffle more to the right on his command, depending on the size of the other divisions involved. We marched onto parade as planned, and after we were halted and facing forward, a guy in an army uniform approached me from the right.

He barked in my ear, "Move back", so that only I could hear. I thought, if anything I was supposed to move sideways, and maybe it was the jitters of having the premier coming to inspect us, but I didn't move. I thought that maybe he would repeat himself thinking that I just didn't hear him. But the second time he gave the order he yelled it so that everyone in attendance could hear, and I could feel his spit landing on my cheek. This time I got the message and moved back, but I can remember feeling very embarrassed.

Once the parade was aligned into its final position; several speeches were made from a podium as we looked on. Then it was announced that the Premier, Ralph Klein, would be inspecting the uniformed members of the parade. We were called to attention as the Premier headed towards us. I was the first person to be inspected. I can remember feeling a little nervous as the Premier approached, but that soon passed as I realized how down to earth Ralph was. He just smiled at me, said "Hi," and then moved on.

After the inspection was complete, we were told there would be food and refreshments available on the other side of the building. Then we were marched off parade. As we marched around the corner of the building I saw my wife beaming at me and I smiled back at her. She was standing with another woman I had not seen before. My attention was broken when I heard a couple of my buddies near me saying, "hey look at those girls, woo hoo". To which I said, "Hey settle down, that's my wife." I was so proud.

After the parade broke, I reunited with my wife and parents. We wandered the grounds for a bit. There were a couple of helicopters on display, and we took some pictures of each of us sitting inside them.   Then we decided to get something to eat. I sat alone with my wife eating lunch while my parents mingled around. We got up from our table because I wanted another burger, but on the way my parents stopped us. They were talking to one of my buddies and I guess they figured I needed to say hello. So as I stopped to talk to my friend Keith my mom pulled out her camera. Then she noticed Ralph Klein standing nearby and started calling him.

The premier heard my mom and turned around. She boldly asked him if she could take his picture with us. He agreed, and then he lined up between my wife and me, with Keith on the outside. I was surprised that this was happening but I thought, way to go mom. Ralph put his arms around my wife and me, and my mom snapped the picture.

The dignitaries make their speeches

Later on I heard a funny story from my wife about what happened during that picture. As Ralph put his arm around her, she went to do the same in return. I guess she must have been a little nervous because she apparently didn't swing her arm back far enough, and as she was lifting her arm she accidentally slapped Ralph on the bottom. Then dying of embarrassment, she just kept her arms at her sides. I wonder what Ralph thought.

The following week, our picture ran in both of the local Sherwood Park newspapers.

CLUB MOORA

In January of 1999, I was sent to Stanley Park, Vancouver, for a Harbour Defense exercise. It was a weekend long training session that included many sailors from all over Western Canada, as well as the few sailors that I had made the trip up with from Edmonton.

During my career in the Reserves, I often spent my evenings in the local bars and pubs with fellow sailors when we were given the night off. This particular time in Gas Town comes to mind.

Before we made the trip out to Vancouver, we all attended a short meeting in Edmonton the Wednesday night before the weekend. This was the typical meeting we're all accustomed to. The one in which they tell us where our accommodations are, what they are like, what time the flight is, when to meet at the airport and so on. At the end of the meeting, the PO who was giving all the instructions mentioned that we should use the buddy system when we go out at night because Gas Town was a rough place.

Nonetheless, we made the trip out that Friday night, and arrived at the local reserve unit Discovery, in Vancouver. As soon as everyone arrived, we were told to meet in Discovery's gym. As we walked in, I saw some faces I had seen before, and some that I hadn't. As many of the sailors recognized one another, conversations and reminiscing ensued. Then the group of officers, who were in charge of coordinating the weekend, got everyone's attention and began to speak. The sailors were then divided into their crews and watch rotations.

After everyone was assigned to their positions, if you weren't on duty, you got the all clear to hit the town. I was lucky enough to get crewed up with a buddy from home. We went to find a couple of the other guys from home to make some plans for the evening. Six of us got together and decided to just catch a ride into Gas Town and wing it from there. But first we had to check the duty roster. It turned out that one of us had duty this night, so the remaining five of us headed out.

We jumped into a cab and drove to Gas Town. The driver dropped us off at a main intersection that was all paved with cobblestones and had a large water fountain in the center of it. There wasn't much vehicular traffic in the area; it was crowded mostly with pedestrians. We all decided to walk around for a bit to get a feel for the area. It didn't take us too long to notice that a strange culture existed here. As we were walking past the fountain a couple of girls were shouting at a guy with a camera to hurry up and take their picture. It was cold enough to see your breath that night, but these two girls were standing knee deep right in the water.   They were staggering around and giggling, but they composed themselves long enough to start passionately kissing each other when the pictures were being taken. Funny thing was the locals didn't seem to notice, I think they were mostly all strung out.

A passerby stopped to ask us if we wanted to buy some pot or mushrooms. Instead we asked him where we could go for a drink. He pointed to a place down the road in the direction we were heading. He said to go upstairs to a place he called club Moora.

We followed his advice and headed for this club. We walked up the stairs and met a nice looking girl at the door who was taking cover charges.   The cover was outrageous and we had second thoughts about going in. We soon decided that it was getting late and we didn't know of another place to go, so in we went.

Once inside the club, we immediately felt all eyes on us. We were the only white guys in the place, amidst a room full of black guys. As we made our way towards the bar we really felt like we were in the wrong place. What the hell did that guy on the street send us in here for, to get us killed?   As I looked at the many pairs of eyes watching me, I could see that they weren't too impressed. It felt as though their world had stopped for these five white guys who came onto their turf.

We got our drinks and sat down, and slowly but surely, they started to ignore us and go back to their routine. I think everyone in there knew each other, and they were all aware of our intrusion. After a while, one of them grabbed a microphone and started rapping. A somewhat muscular gentlemen wearing black leather pants, an open vest with no undershirt, with several gold chains dangling from his neck. You could see the veins popping out in his neck as he paced back and forth furiously while rapping and looking at the crowd with bloodshot eyes.

The dance floor came alive and our table emptied out as well. My buddy Jason and me stayed behind to watch everyone's drinks. I started talking to Jason about something, but I could tell he wasn't listening to me. He looked a little inebriated and his eyes were fixed on a girl sitting at a table across from us. As the girl's eyes panned the room she came across Jason staring at her. She looked away and then looked back seconds later. When she noticed that Jason was still staring at her, she said, "What the fuck are you looking at."

I could tell she was quite pissed off at Jason. And when I looked over at him myself, he was still just staring at her. But it looked as though I could have pushed him out of his chair and he wouldn't have blinked. When I looked back in the girl's direction, there was a rather large guy standing over her. He was staring right at us with looks to kill as she was whispering something in his ear. Suddenly the guy straightened up and signaled to a couple of other guys a few feet away, he was motioning them in our direction.

It seemed as though we could feel guys closing in on us from a few different directions. I told Jason that it was time to make a run for it. For a second I thought I was going to have to pick him up and carry him, but he eventually got to his feet. We walked as calmly as we could through the dance floor, picked up our buddies, and got the hell out of there.

WATCHING THE GATE IN WAINWRIGHT

During the first three-quarters of my career, there was a certain trip that was a favorite of mine, the ever-popular Wainwright weekend. Up until the last few years of my career, I would travel out at least once a year to re-qualify and refresh on my weapons firing skills. The trip usually started with a drive out on a Friday. I always enjoyed the idea of getting paid to drive or sit in a vehicle for a couple of hours with my buddies. I remember how we would stop at the first gas station on our way out of town to load up on junk food for the drive down, and then just reminisce and tell stories the whole way.

We would usually go out on the town on Friday and Saturday nights and drive home on Sunday in the afternoon. The working portion of the weekend consisted of an all-day shoot on Saturday, followed by a half-day shoot on Sunday. There was usually some time mixed in there to clean the weapons after each shooting day ended.

Sadly, this outing gave way to one-day trips to the Edmonton range in the later years of my career. But as I look back fondly on these outings, one particular trip comes to mind.

It was about October of 1997, and I believe it to be my second last trip out that way. There were four of us in the truck, but we were part of a larger convoy that would arrive later by bus. Our vehicle was carrying the rifles, and it was our job to get down there first and prepare the place for the rest of our crew. When we arrived at the base, we stopped off at the main office to sign in and collect our linen and meal cards. Then we were given the keys and directions to our Quonset.

The Quonset was an H-shaped building, at each end there were dorms which were joined in the middle by washrooms, a small laundry area, and a gang shower. There were signs posted above the washbasins and in the drinking fountains that said, "Don't drink the water." As I walked through the washrooms to the other dorm, I found that the door was locked, and so we would all have to share the one dorm. There was enough room in there; the problem was that our crew was mixed gender. So the first thing we decided to do was to make a shower schedule and post it up in the washroom. Then we swept the floor and opened the doors to get some air circulation in the building.

Outside it was a beautiful sunny day, but there was already snow on the ground so we had to shovel the walkway. In the corner by the front door we found some shovels. Then two of us shoveled while the other two emptied all the gear out of the truck and brought it into the building. It felt a little weird, just the four of us in this big open vacant building that was filled with bunk beds, sunlight, and dust. But that night the building would come to life when the rest of the guys got there.

The next thing we did was to choose our beds, make them, and then stow our personal gear in the lockers provided. Then we found a big tarp, which we hung from the ceiling about half way down the dorm to provide a separation between the genders.

After we finished all our work, we used the gun boxes as card tables and we played cards to pass the time until the Chief arrived. The Chief was to arrive with a Petty Officer, the two of them were in charge of the weekend. The four of us were to act as their range staff, we wouldn't be involved in the shoot.

We expected to be allowed to go out for a few drinks when the Chief arrived, but he had different plans for us. We were told to pull out all the weapons and give them a good pre-fire cleaning. Meanwhile the Chief and Petty Officer moved in. They rested for a while, then they got up and left the building. A short time later they returned with some beer and gave us each one. But as our tensions were rising, they finally decided to let us out for a little while. When we returned a couple hours later, the rest of the group had arrived and they were just moving in. A short time later it was lights out.

The next day while the rest of the crew pilled onto the bus, we loaded the truck with our supplies. We drove down to the range where we set up for the shoot. Before we got started, the firing group was assigned to their rotation. They were to shoot in cycles of three, with five shooters on the range at a time. The range staff was assigned to their positions. Two guys at the ammo truck, one would load the ammo, the other would run it back and forth to the firing line. One guy was stationed on the firing line to coach the shooters and clear jammed weapons. The last guy would be down at the gate to stop vehicles and people from entering the range. Members of the range staff were expected to stay at each station for an hour at a time.

Once things got underway, I started off at the ammo truck as the runner. This job wasn't bad, but there was a lot of running back and forth. Once the hour was up, and since there were two of us at the ammo truck, it was up to us to start the rotation. As the runner, I went up to take position on the firing line. With the Chief and PO standing behind me I felt like I was in the spotlight, and so I soon tired of this job. At last the time came for me to go down and man the gate. When I got there the guy joked that he didn't want to be relieved, and asked if I wanted to just go back to the ammo truck. I refused, and soon he was on his way up to the truck.

The first thing I did when I arrived was to get on the radio and report my position to the Chief at the firing point, then I sat down to relax. It was Saturday, so the roads were very quiet, in fact the whole time I was down there I didn't have to stop anybody, although a few cars drove by now and then. I absolutely loved this job; there was no running, and no spotlight. I was free to sit there with my thoughts; this was a nice way to earn money.

All too soon it was nearing the end of my hour. I started to feel the need to go to the washroom, but that was back up the hill near the firing point. I didn't want to radio in and ask for my relief. It was too close to rotation, and I didn't want to remind anyone of this because I enjoyed my job at the gate. So I held it in until I couldn't stand it any more. I walked out of the shack and saw a small burn barrel made out of a culvert pipe standing on end. It stood about one and one half feet high. I walked over to it, then pulled down my pants and leaned over into it and did a number 2 right smack in the middle of it. I was very nervous that somebody would drive by and see me, but at least I was wearing a three-quarter-length parka that provided some privacy.

I quickly pulled up my pants and darted back into the shack. I looked around for something to wipe with but couldn't find anything. Then, there on the wall I saw a bulletin posted up that said, "Keep this room clean," and it was signed by the range safety officer. I removed it from the protective sleeve, and well, you know.

This ended up being all for not because only a few minutes later, my relief came. Later at lunchtime, I ran into the guy who relieved me at the gate. He had a dirty look on his face, then he cracked into a wry smile and shook his head. We both had a good laugh.

REPAIRING THE RHIB ARCH

One of the tools used often by the Reserves is the RHIB rescue boat. These boats are very efficient for search and rescue, man over board, and other evolutions such as securing to a buoy. They can maneuver quite well in the water, and are capable of traveling at fairly high speeds. To drive a RHIB you must complete a two-week training course and be awarded with your RHIB ticket.

I believe these boats are capable of carrying up to twelve people, but I could be wrong on that. They are also equipped with a global positioning system (GPS), a loud hailer, a siren, and a radio. These items are suspended above, and in front of the driver's head. They are part of a large console that is held in place by a stand called the Arch, which is fastened to four hard points on the RHIB using nuts and bolts. The legs of the stand are made of an aluminum piping material that was designed to be as lightweight as possible.

In later years the design of the arch started to come under a lot of scrutiny. Because of the maneuverability of these boats, and certain G-forces from sharp turns and such, the welds on the joints were constantly under stress. Sometimes the welds began to crack; the material was too lightweight to serve its purpose. In fact, one time while I was at the Coast doing a weekend training exercise with these boats, I noticed a half-inch crack in one of the welds before we launched. The harbor was quite choppy that day, and when we returned to the jetty, I saw that the crack had tripled in length. I mentioned it to a supervisor, and we condemned that arch for the rest of the weekend.

After that episode, I tried to tell them that inspecting the structural security of the arch should be included in the pre sail checks of the boat. But an overly ambitious Petty Officer interrupted me and acted as though this was his idea, whatever. I'm not quite sure but I think these arches have now been taken out of service altogether.

However, in the summer of 2001 I was asked to help a fellow sailor repair the arch on the RHIB that belonged to our unit. We had a professional welder in our department, and since I was working as a pipe fitter at the time, I went along to help him. To transport the arch to his welding shop in the city, we just laid it in the boat and strapped it down. Then we hitched it to a Defense vehicle and away we were. There was another guy with us to act as the driver since neither of us had our military drivers license at the time. He was a Master Seaman, I was a Leading Seaman, and the welder was an Able Seaman, but he was the man in charge.

Before we went to the shop, our petty officer asked the welder if he could fix the arch. Our welder gave him a lifelong guarantee. I seemed to think otherwise though, because it didn't matter how well the damn thing was welded, the material was to soft. But I just kept my mouth shut because I knew it was going to be an easy payday.

Once we got to the shop, the Master Seaman lent a hand getting the arch out, and then he just poked around while the welder and me did our thing. The welder cut the arch legs completely apart and put a smaller piece of pipe inside the legs for added structural support. He also added in a couple more gussets where he thought they would be necessary. I did the fit up on the legs while he welded them, making sure not to misalign the boltholes. All in all, the job went pretty smoothly, and the in the end the arch fit the boat like a glove.

It was an easy day of work for us all. I always enjoy it when the Navy needs my civilian skills. We brought back the newly repaired arch and were heroes for the next short while. But as that boat was put in service of few more times, the welds just started peeling off of it in other places. So much for the welder's lifetime guarantee, but I guess it wasn't his fault.

THROWN OVERBOARD

During a week's worth of maintenance at my home unit, I was given word that I would be posted aboard my first Destroyer, the HMCS Kooteney. I was expected to sail aboard the regular force vessel from January 13th to March 26th of 1995 as one of only three reserve augments in a ship's compliment that included over one hundred regular force men and officers.

To the best of my knowledge, reg. force sailors did not like reservists. We were dubbed the weekend warriors and our existence in the forces was looked upon as a hobby, while to them it was a way of life. Because we were part timers we put in less than half the effort they did, and our promotions came with less effort. Our rank was not as respected as theirs; in fact, if a reservist were to transfer over to the reg. forces, he or she would receive a demotion of at least two to three ranks.

I wasn't concerned with the rank structure because at the time I was still just an Ordinary Seaman. But at least my basic training course was the same as theirs, and it was my third year in the forces. However, upon boarding the Kootenay, I planned to act as though I was fresh out of basic training. If I didn't have to tell them I was a reservist, I wasn't going to. Besides, if they knew I had been in the reserves for three years and I was still an Ordinary Seaman they would think there was something wrong with me.

On the night of January the 13th 1995, my plane touched down in Victoria, BC. I had been on a boat before, but nothing of this magnitude. I felt even more alone and scared than I did at seventeen, venturing off to Basic Training.

With nobody to meet me at the airport, I stood alone in line at the baggage carousel waiting for my bag. Armed with only my papers and the name of the ship I was posted to, it felt good to see what became a familiar sight to me over the years in my career. My big green duffel bag with the little piece of paper stuffed in the end that read ### McPherson. The "###" was the last three digits of my social security number. When I was in basic training we were all told to mark our bags in this manner, and though that piece of paper became yellow and faded, it never left my duffel bag. I guess I left it there to forever remind me of my humble beginnings, a time when everyone was just a number.

With my duffel bag and papers in hand, I ventured outside the airport. I had a quick cigarette and then took a cab to the dockyard. When we reached the main gates the Commissioner asked to look at my military I.D., then he gave the cab driver directions to the ship and waived us through.

Driving the HMCS Kootenay

I can remember pulling up to the ship and looking at it from the cab. What a spectacle she was, floating there secured to the dock against the backdrop of a quiet Victoria night sky. For a brief moment I wished that I could just turn around and go home, thinking to myself what have I gotten into now. However, I paid the driver, got my receipt, and stepped out of the cab.

The ship was a bustle of activity. Usually when a ship is along side at nighttime, most of the sailors leave or go home and only a small crew called the duty watch stay behind to man the boat. But as I arrived, the duty watch was participating in a practice fire drill and it seemed to me there were quite a few sailors running around.

As I walked across the brow of the ship I felt a little stupid standing there with my luggage and papers in hand, and not in uniform. It seemed as though nobody saw me walk onto the ship, and I was looking for the best place to stand out of the way of all the activity. Luckily, I arrived just as the fire drill was wrapping up. Some of the sailors were gathering up fire hoses and other equipment, while others were taking off their fire fighting suits and breathing devices. I noticed one or two of them occasionally looking at me, which made me think I should be helping them. Instead I just wished in my head that they would hurry up so I could find someone to report to.

Once all the gear was stowed away, the sailors formed up in three ranks and were given a brief description from a couple of officers on how they did, what they could have done better, and so on. Then almost as suddenly as one of the officers said "Dismissed," sailors went scurrying and disappeared down and through the various doors and hatches. In a short instant you could hear the gentle rippling of the water as it splashed against the side of the ship.

I approached a Petty Officer to introduce myself and hand over my papers. He was a little intimidating but I sensed it was just for show. After we discovered that I was in his department, he told me not to take any shit from these guys and brought me over to an Able Seaman who was manning the phones. When I was introduced I could tell he couldn't care less about me. The PO told him to page another sailor to the brow to show me around. The next sailor, an Able Seaman as well, seemed to be a bit friendlier. When he arrived at the brow, he snapped to attention in a joking manner that let me know he had a little more personality than the other guy.

I went along with him to see the rest of the ship. He was a nice enough guy, but at the same time I could tell he was hardly interested in me either. Whenever I thought of something appropriate or funny to say, he would agree without emotion and then continue talking about the compartments on the boat and so on. He showed me the front end of the ship first. This was where our department slept and hung out most of the time. When I met with the few guys that were there, I got the same warm welcome that I did from the Able Seaman on the upper decks manning the phone. The impression that I got from these guys is that I should basically keep my mouth shut and do what I was told. I was then informed that there were no more beds, and I was going to have to stay at the back of the ship with the Stokers. Little did I know it then, but there was a known rivalry between our trades.

I was led to the back of the ship, then down a ladder into the Stoker's cabin, which housed about 20 sailors. They were a strange bunch of guys that usually lived in darkness in the after cabin because of their shift work. The guy I was with asked the Stokers if they had any empty beds. They pointed at one that was the top bunk out of three. Most of the beds, except for mine, had curtains draped around them for privacy.

My tour guide decided to leave as the Stoker's showed me where my locker was. It was just around the corner from my rack in a small corridor that had lockers on both sides and was wide enough for just one person to walk through at a time. Because there were no lights back there, you had to have a flashlight to see anything, and you had to crouch slightly to get in there. I began to stow my gear. First I would lay it out on my bed, which was about face level. Then I would squeeze down my items little by little, and crawl around the corner to my locker to put it away. Thank God we weren't sailing right away, and most of the other sailors were ashore and out of the way. When I would have to use my locker, the quarters were so tight that I would literally be leaning on the locker behind me with my feet straddled a little to be able to stand shorter.

After I was finished stowing all my gear, I went back up the ladder and down the flats to the main cafeteria. There I met a young Ordinary Seaman from my department who seemed to take an interest in me. It looked as though things were starting to look up. I went out onto the upper decks to have a quick cigarette before bed.

When I crawled into bed I discovered that it was only about 6 to 8 inches wider than me, which left only a couple of inches on either side when I was laying flat. My feet hung over the edge slightly, and if I put my elbow on my stomach, my fist would touch firmly against the deck head above. You could not sit up in bed, there was only enough room to crawl in or out. The beds were equipped with a personal light that swung in from the side, and there was a small bedside storage space. It measured about 6 inches by 6 inches and ran the entire length of the bed. Sleeping in these conditions was something to get used to, especially when the ship was out to sea.

Relaxing in the cafeteria

As time went on I began to get into the routine of life on a large warship. I kept mostly to myself, minded my own business, and went about my duties in a professional manner. Until one day, about two weeks into my time onboard, a chance arose for me to fit in with my department. We were all gathered in the sitting area of the Boatswains mess when some of the guys decided that at lunchtime we would all sit at the Stoker's table. I thought sure, this sounds like a harmless prank and I decided to go along with it.

When lunchtime came we carried on with our plan. The Stokers were baffled; they didn't seem to know what to make of us sitting at their table. Even though there were other places to go and sit, they were so used to sitting at this one particular table that they just kind of stood around. Some of them just leaned up against the bar that was right beside us and ate their lunch. It was kind of funny and I didn't think too much of it at the time.

A couple of nights later, I was on watch until 4 O'clock in the morning. After my watch was over, I went down into the Stoker's mess where I was staying. It was pitch dark and dead silent down there. I stumbled around a bit until I found my flashlight. I found my way to my locker and then I took off my uniform and slipped a towel around my waist. I slid my feet into my shower thongs, collected up my toiletries, and then headed back up top for a quick shower before bed. The shower was nice and relaxing, it felt great after a cold and rainy night on the upper decks. I quickly brushed my teeth and headed back down below to bed.

When I got back down below into the Stoker's mess, I found that it was still as dark and quiet as it was when I had left for my shower. I went to make a quick stop off at my locker to put my things away. I leaned against the locker behind me, clad in just my towel and shower thongs, and opened my locker with the key I kept around my neck. Suddenly a light turned on to my left; it sort of made me jump a little. Then a large figure loomed towards me, and as he stepped into the light I could see that he too was clad in just a towel. He came toward me and said, "Hi". I was a little startled because he just seemed to come out of nowhere and I had not seen anyone else in the showers, but I quickly assumed that he was probably just going to his locker for something. I returned his hello and turned to my right to go to my bed. He quickly turned the other way, walked around the lockers, and met me on the other side. Now I knew something was up, my heart began to race. With everyone else asleep, this didn't seem like a situation where you could yell for help.

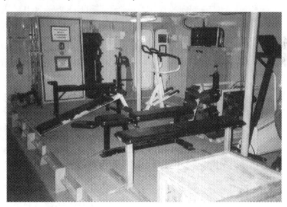

The ship's weight room

The sailor was about 6'4", and probably weighed 240lbs. I was only 19 years old, just young and scared. He asked me how I was doing. I told him I was a little tired and that I just wanted to go to bed. I really had no other place to go, and in my head I was pleading that this person would just leave me alone. I started walking towards my bed and I noticed that he started to follow me, at that point I was really starting to feel homesick. When we got to my bed, I turned around to tell him again that I was just going to go to sleep. Suddenly, he grabbed my arm rather firmly, and his tone got a little more serious as he said, "Come with me."

My first reaction was to try to break free of this man's grasp and pull my arm away. I gave a slight tug hoping that would be enough, but it wasn't. Then a second person emerged from the darkness and grabbed hold of my other arm. The two men started escorting me into the TV area that was blocked off with a curtain. As we came closer, I noticed from the gap at the bottom of the curtain that the light was on. One of my captors held the curtain aside while the other pushed me into the room. Once inside, I was confronted by at least a half a dozen sailors not including the two who had brought me in there.

One of the sailors was holding a video camera, and he was taping the whole event from the moment I came into the room. The other sailors were holding bed sheets and duct tape. I tried to turn around and push the guys at the door out of the way, but three or four of them grabbed me right away. They told me that they could make things hard or easy for me, depending on how much I was going to struggle with them. I was terrified, but I decided to heed their warning and not put up a fight.

They started to wrap the sheets around me while I was standing up with my arms at my sides. Then came the duct tape, which they applied quite liberally. There were places on my legs that weren't covered by the sheets, but the duct tape was wrapped firmly around them regardless. I was very nervous and breathing quite heavily, and as I was exhaling, they put a couple good tight wraps across my chest. The feeling of each breath being cut shorter was causing me a lot of panic. So I yelled, "I can't breathe." To which they replied, "You'll be alright," and proceeded to try to lift me off my feet. At the time I weighed about 200 pounds, and they had much difficulty lifting me. At one point, one of the guys carrying me at the shoulders just about fell down and I could here a couple of chairs sliding across the deck in the commotion. I was hoping that this would play to my advantage and that they would just give up on doing whatever it was they were going to do to me.

However, they managed to pick me up and they started to carry me out of the TV room towards the ladder, which was angled at about 70 degrees. They proceeded to carry me up the ladder feet first, and their determination put a new fear into my head. Were they going to throw me overboard? It was the middle of the night and our ship was steaming along to some destination. Nobody on my crew would notice that I was gone for at least another 4 hours. In that amount of time our ship would be long gone.

My worries about this were cut short briefly as one of the sailors carrying my right shoulder lost his grip when we were at least half way up the ladder. I dangled briefly with no way to brace my own fall. Thankfully the sailor regained his grip, at last a slight moment of relief. However it was not too comforting to smell the rum on his breath as he was standing over me.

And so they continued to carry me up the ladder until we reached the top. They were all exhausted; so they set me down to have a quick rest. I was tired as well just because of the whole ordeal, so I just enjoyed the rest myself. As I was lying there, I tried to think of what I would do if these guys brought me to the ladder leading to the upper decks. I planned to just save my energy until then, and I was going to go crazy on them when the time came.

They picked me up, this time with less of a struggle, and the adventure was on again. They proceeded to carry me down the flats passing the turn leading to the upper decks. What a relief, they didn't round that corner. They continued to carry me until we were at the front end of the ship where my department sleeps. They brought me into the TV area, threw me down onto the couch, and then left.

I laid there in the quietness for a couple of seconds. Once I realized this was the end of the prank I began yelling for someone to help get the tape and sheets off of me. The guys from my department came in to help me out. They didn't seem too happy that I had woken them from their sleep, and they started ripping the tape off of me. All the while I was complaining that the hair on my legs was being pulled out.

When the whole ordeal was done, the guys told me to go back down to the Stoker's cabin and go to sleep. So with my legs all red and sore, and feeling very humbled, I sheepishly went back down to 11 mess and quietly went to bed. What a day!

PLUMBING AT NONSUCH

In June of 1997, I began my civilian career as a plumber. As time went on, people at my Reserve unit began to catch wind of this. It wasn't long before I began doing side jobs in the homes of fellow sailors. I also answered a lot of plumbing related questions, and gave a few tips now and again. I liked being thought of as the Unit's resident plumber.

When I had to address plumbing problems at our unit, I liked the idea that suddenly my superiors had to listen to me when I would fix the problem. I would be the one giving the orders and taking the credit for a job well done. Actually, my skills as a plumber helped when it came time for my superiors to write my yearly evaluations. It was always a factor on those evaluations that I routinely helped with ongoing maintenance issues at the Unit.

One time during a Wednesday training night in the fall of 2001, I was told that the water fountain in the gymnasium wasn't draining properly.   It had been previously listed as out of order, and temporarily fixed with drain cleaner by the Unit's maintenance man.   Since we were wearing our number one uniform that evening, they told me that I could fix it the next night I was in.   I'm the type of guy who doesn't like to put things off.   So I immediately took off my jacket, rolled up my sleeves, and got down to business.   There was a sailor helping me who was a Master Seaman, but I was telling him what to do.

I needed a screwdriver to take the fountain apart, so I went over to the Engineer's department to borrow one.   That's when I caught shit from the Chief for not wearing my jacket.   I just agreed with him thinking to myself, "whatever".   He didn't realize I was busy doing a job for the Unit, but I didn't care to tell him either.   I got the screwdriver and went back to complete my project.   As I was once again working on the fountain, and beginning to draw a crowd, I noticed the Chief watching me from across the gym.

I completed the job and I had just finished putting the fountain back together when the Chief and the Unit's Commanding Officer approached me.   In a rare military moment, I received a pat on the back from the CO.   But she urged me to at least put on some coveralls the next time.

A few months later, around Christmas 2001, during a mess meeting in the Junior Ranks bar, it was brought to my attention that the dishwasher wasn't working properly. I opened the dishwasher to take a quick look at it.   There was a couple inches of water inside, and various mold spores clung to it's interior. I assumed that this might just be a drainage problem. But remembering what I had gone through with the water fountain, I agreed to come in and have a look at it on a Monday night.

Monday night came and I signed in for a half days pay. I hadn't officially gotten the OK to come in so I signed the roster while nobody was around. But since the breaker panel outside the bar was not labeled, I was caught when I shut off the breaker for the office computers. I caught shit from my divisional officer this time, but it was agreed that I could continue. It turned out that the drainpipes were in good condition. It was the dishwasher that was broken. When I told this to the mess president she asked if I could fix the problem. I told her she needed to buy a new dishwasher.

I also told her that I had just bought myself a new one and I had a second hand one for sale in the "Bargain Finder". I offered to donate my old dishwasher, providing I could come in on a Saturday and install it for a full days pay. She told me to hold it until the new year, which I did. I turned down a lot of calls for that dishwasher until my ad stopped running. When I returned to the Unit in the new year, I was told an officer was questioning my half days pay because I did not fix the dishwasher and they didn't want my old one, what a slap in the face.

There was another mess meeting held to decide how much money the mess members were willing to spend on a new dishwasher from the mess funds. Someone had done some price shopping, and a new dishwasher would cost around $600.00. I just sat back and laughed when the members started to say, "I thought we were getting Cam's old one". Then they had the gonads to ask if I would do the installation if they bought a new one. I told them to get stuffed. By the end of the training year (May 2002), they still hadn't bought a new dishwasher. I guess they had better things to spend money on. At the start of the next training year that fall, the old dishwasher was still there, ha ha.

BASE DEFENSE

During my career there were a few times when I was involved with a base defense force at my home unit, HMCS Nonsuch. I remember the first one I did around 1993, which seemed more like a hostage taking. There was a point in time when we were all in the junior ranks mess and the supposed enemy had surrounded the building. One of our guys got a little carried away when he booted the back door open, came flying out screaming, and did an awkward dive roll while pretending to shoot at the enemy. I think the guy caught shit later on for his "Rambo" impression. An outburst like that was not what the instructors were looking for.

The next time I took base defense training, it was a little more sophisticated. We had Military Police instructing the course instead of our own guys who thought they knew what they were doing. There were more lectures and learning to do this time before we tried another real time exercise all half cocked. We learned the art of take downs and body searches inside the building in slow time with the instructors giving close details while we practiced on each other. After we did enough practice, they sent half of our guys out of the room. When they came back, we were told that one of them had a concealed weapon on them and we were supposed to find it. The guys kept concealing their weapon right by their genitals of course, thinking that the searcher wouldn't check there. But the MP's kept encouraging us to check thoroughly because in real life, thoroughness was the difference between life and death.

Then the MP's got out a box of latex gloves and passed them around. They said it was time to learn about body cavity searches. My heart went into my throat as I thought; they're not going to make us practice this are they? Fortunately it was just a joke, and the MP's had a good laugh at our expense.

The next day, the rest of our unit was scheduled to come in for non-related training. We set up roadblocks entering the unit as a way to practice vehicle searches. As shocked members of our unit arrived for training, we would stop them and ask for ID. Apparently, at any time there was supposed to be an MP coming through in civilian clothing.

When the plain clothed MP tried to gain access through our gates, we stopped him to ask for ID. When he didn't have any, we had him step out of the vehicle while we searched it. One of our guys who was supposed to be watching the MP while we conducted our search, made a vital mistake. He took his eyes off the suspect for only a short moment. He soon found himself in a headlock, with his gun taken away. At this point, the scenario ended so the MP's could tell us what went wrong. It was a good thing they ended the scenario too, because we had civilians looking on wondering if this was real.

In the next scenario, we had a woman pretending to be pregnant. One of our young Medical Aids was told to assess her condition, because we were not going to let her into the building. The lady started to scream in pain, and she wouldn't let the Med Aid come close to her. She was lying on the ground screaming and crying for help hysterically. She was starting to have a lot of us convinced that this was not part of the exercise. This time we had onlookers poking out of the nearby hotel yelling at us to help the lady. Finally we gave her access into the building, that's when we learned we made a mistake.

That weekend was a very fun and informative weekend for me. But when our unit decided to have another weekend like this a few years later, I made it my last. We had the MP's working as the bad guys again, but our leaders decided once again that they would conduct the training. Once again this training commenced on the night before a regularly scheduled training day for the rest of the unit. We were told that we would be sleeping over at the unit on cots. Well, they never gave us a damn bit of sleep that night and they kept sending us outside for surveillance. We were supposed to be on a watch rotation, but every time I lay down to sleep the alarm was raised that there was trouble outside.

When I was on watch throughout the wee hours of the morning freezing my nuts off, nothing happened. The next morning we all looked like the walking dead when the rest of our unit arrived for the training day. I thought we would be allowed to get some sleep, but they told us to go join our departments and get to work. We were furious, and we talked about filing a grievance before finally being granted the chance to leave at noon. I was lucky enough to make the drive home without falling asleep.

YAG WEEKEND AT MOLLY'S REACH

Nearing the end of my first year in the reserves, from March 31st to April 04th of 1993, I went on my second trip aboard a YAG. A YAG, which stands for Yard Auxiliary Gate, is a small vessel used primarily to train junior officers in navigation, and for the men it was a chance to learn how to drive a boat as well as a few of the basics. I'm not sure how many YAG's there are in the fleet, but they all seemed to be built a little different from one another. They all had one level below the upper decks, and this was divided into two cabins with separate ladders leading to each. The first YAG I sailed on 6 months earlier, only slept about 16 sailors, twelve in the back and four in the front. In addition to having the four bunks up forward, there was also a small dining area, and a tiny kitchen behind three walls. There were no showers on that YAG, and there was only one washroom, which was located in the after cabin.

There were instructions posted on how to operate the toilet because it had to be hand pumped in order to flush.

This YAG however, was slightly larger than the first, and had room to house a few more sailors. The forward cabin included tiny separate sleeping quarters for the few females we had onboard. It had a private door and it was located in the forward cabin instead of a kitchen. The kitchen was on the upper decks under the canopy at the top of the ladder leading into the forward cabin. And the other thing that made this YAG better than the first is that it was equipped with a shower, also located on the upper decks.

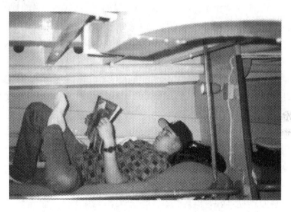

Relaxing in my "rack"

During this voyage it was learned that we were going to visit the town that was made famous by the TV series, the Beachcombers. Along the way the crew practiced a few drills including fighting a fire onboard the ship, as well as a few man over board rescues. One lunch hour, I overheard a crewmember telling a story about the last time he came out that way. He said that during shore leave one night, he and some of the boys were wandering around the docks and found Relic's boat. They had been drinking, and as the story goes, one of them decided to take a piss in the boat. The guy telling the story was laughing his head off, but I think they probably pissed in the wrong boat.

When we finally arrived at our destination, we had to do a quick cleaning of the boat once we had her docked. We also hooked up to shore power and took all our garbage ashore. Then we had a meeting in the forward cabin while supper was being made. After supper, it was time for a wash up, and then a trip to shore.

It was pretty much decided that we would all stick together as a group and go to the same pub. The pub we went to had two levels. On the ground level there was a large area half filled with tables, and the other half was a dance floor with a small stage for the band. Upstairs there were two pool tables and a balcony that overlooked the first level. Our group consisted of crews from two other YAG's, so there were quite a few of us. We pulled a bunch of tables together and then most of the younger crewmembers, including myself, went upstairs to play pool.

There was a young couple with a friend playing at one table, and we pretty much had the other table for most of the night. I played a few games until the beer started catching up to me. After that, I just sat at one of the side tables with a few of the boys. We talked and drank and smoked for hours until little by little, our crowd started migrating downstairs to join the larger group. Soon there was just me and a buddy sitting there, until he told me he had to go to the washroom. He said he was coming back and he left his pack of smokes on the table. So I just sat there watching the local couple and their friend playing pool until I figured that my buddy wasn't coming back.

Dockyard at Molly's Reach

I got up to go downstairs myself, but when I reached the top of the stairs I was spun around and grabbed by the collar. It was the stranger who was playing pool at the other table. He had my back to the staircase, which was exceptionally long, and he was shaking me violently while insisting that I stole his cigarettes off one of the tables. His girlfriend was pleading with him to let me go but I could see that he must have snapped and wasn't fazed by her screams. I was a little startled and in shock at first, but I shook it off to look very annoyed as I told the guy, "I didn't touch your smokes buddy." But I had a good idea that someone in our group must have taken them. He seemed to snap out of it but he told me I had five minutes to go and get him some smokes from the vending machine downstairs, then he let me go.

I went down the stairs feeling very shaky from my adrenaline rush. The vending machine was right at the bottom of the stairs. When I got to it and looked back up the stairs, the guy had resumed playing pool. So I just walked past the machine and went to our table. There were only three of our guys left and it was close to closing time. I went over and told the boys what happened upstairs. A few moments later, the four of us went back upstairs to confront the guy. It looked as though the tables had turned on him.

Three of us waited back near the stairs and kept an eye on the guy's friend while our biggest guy walked over to him. They talked for a bit, and then they came towards us. I could see the guy was a little scared this time. When they approached, he told me that his problem was just with me and that we should go outside to settle it. I felt ready, but before I could agree to this, my buddies told him that wasn't going to happen and that he had better take his friends and beat a hasty retreat out of there.

Then feeling defeated, he took his friends and walked by us with his head down. I breathed a sigh of relief and thanked my buddies. This was one of those times when it felt good to belong to this organization.

BOAT SHOW IN COLD LAKE

In September of 2000, I went on a boat training excursion to the Cold Lake facility. I had been there for training the previous year and the year before that. There was a Petty Officer from my unit who had moved out that way to support his wife's teaching career. Apparently he met her when she had a brief career in the Reserves, almost before my time. Although I can't remember seeing her at the Unit as a member.

As the story goes, he was a Master Seaman, and she was a Leading Seaman. At the time, I would have been an Ordinary Seaman returning home from basic training. Nowadays, I see them together at Unit functions, he in his full rigs, and she in her civilian attire. I guess he retired from his civilian job when she pursued her career in Cold Lake, but he kept his career in the Reserves as a hobby job.

To keep active at the Unit, the Petty Officer organized boat-training exercises in his new hometown. To me these weekends were the answer to the lost "Wainwright weekends". A new road trip, a place we didn't have to take to the skies to get to. This particular weekend though, was the climax to the "Cold Lake Weekend", because it was the last. After that, road trips became much longer as our new haunt became various lakes in and around Saskatchewan.

However, I will always remember the accommodations at Cold Lake, as they were the best I ever had in the military. It did not matter what rank you were; the rooms were like being at a hotel. They were private, with the exception of a shared bathroom, and they had maid service.

Each room had it's own bar fridge, telephone, TV with remote control, plus an alarm clock. Also, the rooms seemed to be newer than any other places I have stayed in, and the whole base was a lot nicer, and cleaner than any other. I always enjoyed my stays at Cold Lake.

On this particular weekend, we were there to perform a boat show for the local residents and media. This was the only boat show I had taken part in during my career, and I remember feeling like a mini celebrity on the way there. So that night, before any boating had even taken place, me and the boys decided to go to the local mess to celebrate our impending fame the next day. We played pool and took turns buying pitchers of beer until the mess closed in the wee hours of the morning.

Prior to this weekend, I hadn't had a drink for at least a few months. So when I woke up the next morning, I knew I had overdone it. Getting myself together and making my appearance down at the mess hall that morning was one of the toughest moments in my career. When you're in the company of military people, you don't want anyone to know you're hung over. I ordered some bacon and eggs for breakfast, and I remember wanting to die while waiting in line. I sat down with my breakfast and did my best to force most of it down. Everyone around me seemed so cheerful and ready to get out there. I tried to exude the same amount of excitement, but I probably displayed all the personality of a wet napkin.

Once outside the fresh air felt nice, but it was time to take the trucks and boats over to the lake. When we arrived at the lake I tried to hide in the back of the truck and sleep, but that plan only worked for about 5 minutes. It was time to go inside the conference room of the Marina for a briefing on the day's events. Once inside, the Petty Officer looked at me and asked if I was OK. I just brushed it off and said "I'm fine," and I poured myself a coffee, which I had a hard time drinking. The meeting went on, and the newsgirl listened intently and took notes.

The boat show didn't start for a couple of hours, so we had time to get out there and practice some high-speed maneuvers. We were assigned to our boats and we spent a couple of minutes meeting our crewmembers before getting out on the water. The driver from my boat was a sailor out of the Calgary unit, and I was told that he was a crazy driver who was absolutely fearless of death. "Oh goody," I thought to myself as I looked out at the very choppy waters. I could feel my stomach start turning already.

We took to the water; it wasn't too bad at first because we were traveling very slowly out of the docking area. But as soon as we past the breakwater, our driver pushed the throttle all the way down, "Gulp". At full speed we raced headlong towards these monstrous waves with the majority of the crew screaming. My stomach was in my throat, and I don't think I was breathing until we hit that first wave. In an instant, we went from seeing this huge wave loom towards us, to seeing nothing but the cloudy, gloomy sky above us. There was the sickening sound of the motor cavitating to let you know the boat was now air borne. When the boat starts to come back down, it is almost straight up and down in the air because it is heaviest at the back end. Going up the wave feels OK, but coming but down you feel a sense of weightlessness in which your stomach climbs into your chest. Nobody is strapped in, and you have to hold certain muscles stiff to prepare for each crushing landing.

After surviving the first wave the screams filled the air once again, and it was less than a second before we were once again air bourne. We crashed against these waves relentlessly for what seemed like an eternity. In those moments I forgot about feeling sick as I was concentrating on preparing my body for each punishing landing. Suddenly, I had a bad landing and I was off balance. Then the landings got worse and worse and I started to feel a sense of doom, something was going to get broken. I was sitting at the front end of the boat where the driver couldn't see me, and it was too dangerous to get up to get his attention. It was too hard for him too hear me either, so I just hung on the best I could and hoped for the best. My muscles were getting tired, and I wasn't sure how much longer I could last.

Luckily enough for me the ride came to an end. The driver had to stop when one of the girls riding in the back with him smoked her face on the cross bar during a landing and received a black eye. We went back to the Marina to let her off. I got off to go to the washroom because my breakfast was coming up. But before I left the guys at the boat, I put on a tough guy show and told them the ride was pretty tame and I would be ready for more after I went for a quick crap.

Once I got up the hill, I went straight for the washroom and not a moment too soon. I immediately began puking my face off as soon as I got in there. But every time I heard someone coming in, I quickly got up off the floor and sat on the toilet so that no one would know I was sick. I was feeling a lot better, so I went back down to the boat for some more punishment. When I started coming back down the hill toward the boat, the crew cheered. I guess from the comments I had made earlier, they thought I was some kind of maniacal daredevil so I raised my arm in triumph and wiped my mouth with my other sleeve while stumbling towards them.

Once again, we endured another hell ride, and once again I went back up the hill to be sick. I chalked this one up as my worst hangover experience ever. Before going back down to the boats, I went into the Marina to get a drink. Once inside, I overheard the Petty Officers talking to the newsgirl. The boat show was about to start, but someone forgot to pack an extra floater suit for her. Seizing the opportunity, I graciously offered to donate mine. To them, I selflessly took myself out of the show so it could gain media coverage; I was the hero of the moment. To me, there was no damn way I was going back out there, so I wished her good luck and sat down to recuperate.

At the end of the day, every one of my muscles ached and I didn't make the boat show. But at least nobody knew how sick I was.

WABAMUN WEEKEND

In the early part of my career, our unit owned a couple of cabins down at Lake Wabamun. We referred to them as Nonsuch 2. We used this facility to train our junior sailors to drive the various rescue boats. These boats included Zodiacs, Whalers, and one other speedboat we owned that wasn't really an official rescue boat. But we used it for training anyway.

Nonsuch sold off those cabins sometime in the mid to late 90's, and after that we took the odd day trip out that way. But in the days of camping out there, we mostly trained with Zodiacs. In those times, the Zodiac was the main rescue boat used on Reserve ships, and it was good to keep polishing your skills on it.

When I first joined the Navy, the Whalers were still in service. The Whaler is a large canoe-like boat in which you have guys paddling on both sides. I did one training weekend involving these Whalers before they were taken out of service a year or so later.

That was my first weekend at Wabamun sometime in 1992, and I remember it well. The group of us that went out there were all fresh out of basic training, and we had not yet learned to relax. When we got to the cabin, there was a Master Seaman who reminded me of a basic training instructor. He told the Leading Seaman to take us out and make sure there was no horsing around. I wasn't used to anything different yet, so this guy didn't bother me.

Once we rowed out into the middle of the lake, the Leading Seaman told us to put our paddles down. He then took off his life jacket and put it behind his head like a pillow. After a few minutes, the rest of us did the same; it was a beautiful afternoon. We spent the day laughing and telling jokes. When we got back to the cabin, the Master Seaman asked us if the Leading Seaman taught us anything or if he just fooled around. We looked around at each other, and then we told him we had learned something from the Leading Seaman, ha, ha, ha.

Another time when I was out at the lake, this time as a Leading Seaman myself, I wanted to treat the young guys the same way I was treated my first time out. When we arrived at camp, it was starting to get dark. So after we stowed our gear, we made a quick run to the local liquor store, and then lit up a nice campfire. I was told by the two Petty Officers that I would be in charge of the campfire duty watch and that none of the junior sailors on duty were allowed to drink. I assembled my duty watch together to decide who would take each watch. I told them what the PO's said about drinking, but I said they could have a couple each as long as they kept it hidden.

That turned out to be a mistake on my part because they all got wasted and I caught shit for the whole thing. The next day on the water I let everyone drive right away. In the other boats I could see the Leading Seaman driving still, but we were the fun boat. I let one girl drive, a petite little thing who could barely see over the dash, that was a little scary. But the scariest moment came when I was back in control of the boat. I had the throttle all the way down, and we were going as fast as we could. Another Zodiac was screaming towards us at top speed as well. Out of pure luck, we both peeled off in different directions, narrowly missing a deadly collision. When it was happening, there was another Leading Seaman on our boat standing behind me. He was screaming and digging his fingernails into my shoulders. The feeling of wanting to pull over and punch him in the mouth was probably what saved us.

In later years, we rarely went to Lake Wabamun. The last time we went out, we brought our unit RHIB. I was in one of the dispatch boats, and I was supposed to follow the RHIB out to do some navigation. Well, the dispatch boat can't keep up to the RHIB, so they lost us. While we were searching for them, the PO on my boat wanted to drive. He got us stuck in a sand bar. Luckily we managed to get out of it and get back to the dock for lunch. That's when I caught shit for going missing. Then one of the guys on our crew piped up about driving onto the sand bar. I caught shit again for that too. I told them that the PO was driving when it happened, but that didn't help matters. They told me that I was in charge of the boat, and I wasn't supposed to let anyone else drive. Oh well, I never did another trip on that lake after that anyway.

APRIL 28th MEMORIAL

It was April 17th 2002, one of those days that you will always remember where you were at the time. At the conclusion of a training night at Nonsuch, while I was in the mess playing a few games of foosball as I usually do before going home, someone had turned on the bar TV to the CNN news. Immediately, there was an awed hush over the bar. Sailors, men and women alike sat transfixed in, what was to me, the most somber moment I have ever experienced in my military career.

The breaking news was coming from Afghanistan, where tragically four of our fellow service men had met untimely deaths in the service of our Country. Usually, we could play foosball even if the building was falling down around us. But the images coming through the TV screen that night hit home. There were guys staring in disbelief wondering, "Were any of the dead or injured soldiers somebody that I knew?" But regardless of knowing them or not, there was a profound sense and feeling that we lost four close brothers and it honestly gave me chills.

As the news broke, the identities of the men were unclear. But I could remember thinking, by the grace of God, let there be no fatherless children from this tragedy. As I drove home that night thinking of my two children, I thanked those men for their sacrifices, and I promised not to forget them.

Our unit does its weapons training at the Edmonton base, and it is possible we may have at some point met some of these brave men. I know that in the aftermath, I wished that I had. The descriptions of these men in the following weeks told of four incredible young men that would have enriched anyone's life. My heart went out to the beautiful young women they left behind, and I thank them as well for their sacrifice.

As the week went on, the papers were full of these guys, and I felt compelled to be a part of the memorial service. I didn't know at first if I would be able to attend, it depended on how private the ceremony would be. But I had heard it was going to be a full military ceremony, and I figured that since I had a uniform to wear, maybe I could attend. I remember calling home from work to ask my wife to call the base and tell them our situation and ask if we could attend. She was told to just keep reading the papers and wait. They told her that there was such a public outpouring of sympathy that the service might just be open to the public. They were keeping their fingers crossed at the prospect that the Sky Reach Center might be donated by the people of Northlands to act as the venue.

It turned out that the coliseum was going to be donated, so I decided to ask more of my family to come join my wife and me. My sister, who couldn't make it, offered to watch our kids. So on April 28th 2002, my mother, stepfather, brother, sister-in-law, wife, and myself went to the memorial. It had been some time since we all got dressed up to go anywhere together, and this seemed like an excellent way to spend the day together. I can remember feeling so proud to be waiting in line for the bus wearing my uniform. The city bus services ran shuttles free of charge to the memorial, and there were a lot of people waiting at our stop.

When we got on the bus, there were a lot of people in all sorts of different uniforms, and my brother sat with me asking what each uniform was. When we arrived at the stadium my family was sent to the second level, and my wife and I were allowed to go down to the first level because I was in uniform. Instead we opted to all sit together on the upper level.

The service was exceptional, people laughed, cried, and felt patriotic. I was absolutely honored, and thankful to have been a part of it all. Afterwards, the six of us went out for a couple of drinks before going home. We talked to each other about what parts of the service were touching and such. I remember my mom saying she felt choked up when they wheeled one of the soldiers in on a stretcher.

It was definitely a proud day to be a Canadian. My ten-year anniversary was just six days away, so when were having our drinks my family toasted me and congratulated me on my service. I couldn't have asked for a better way to celebrate.

My wife Kellie and me

WEDDING AT NONSUCH

In June of 1998, I became engaged to the most beautiful woman I have ever known; my darling wife Kellie. To this day, Kellie remains the focal point of all my inspiration. She is the one true love of my life, and from the moment I laid eyes on her, I knew I had found the one.

We had planned to be married the following summer at my parent's acreage, but nearing the end of the year we got some news that would change everything. We found out in November that Kellie was pregnant with our first child. Kellie decided that she didn't want to have our wedding next summer because it would be too far into the pregnancy. Instead we had to work quickly on the plans for a shotgun wedding. Kellie decided that we would aim as close to Valentine's day as possible, so we came up with February 13th 1999 as the date.

At the time we were just scraping by, living from check to check in our civilian jobs. Kellie had a part time job as a hairdressser, and I was an apprentice plumber. We didn't have a heck of a lot of money so we had to try to do things with as little cost as possible.

The biggest detail I stressed over was where were we going to have the wedding? Then one night while I was down at my Reserve unit, somebody heard me discussing this problem to a buddy of mine. From there it was suggested that I use our Reserve Unit's building. I was told that people had done so before, and this included past weddings. I was also told that for members, there was no rental fee, so I immediately called home to tell my wife I found the place.

The bride arrives

Kellie was ecstatic, because when we were dating, I had brought her to Nonsuch before for formal dinners, so she was able to start imagining how we would decorate right away. Nonsuch had it's own bar, so we wouldn't have to worry about stocking up on liquor supplies, or worry about who would run the bar. Also, it was decided that I would just wear my uniform instead of renting a tuxedo. Suddenly everything seemed easy.

The next training night at Nonsuch, I went down to the ship's office to sign out the building for that day in February. The Petty Officer I talked to, told me that there was no longer free rental for the building and that I had just missed the cut off. It was going to cost us $300.00, and on top of that she told me that we would have to hire a duty watch of at least five people including an officer and a bartender. My heart sank, paying for the duty watch would be over $500.00 in wages alone, and with the cost of the building rental thrown in there it just wasn't feasible. I told the PO not to fill out the paperwork just yet, I would have to go back and discuss things with my wife. It looked like we were back to square one.

But as I walked away from the ship's office with a heavy heart, an officer who heard the whole story told me that he would volunteer to be at my wedding, and that if I asked around he was sure I could get the rest of the crew I needed. Suddenly, $300.00 for the building seemed like a deal to me now. I went back to the Junior Ranks mess where I was able to enlist the rest of the guys I would need. They all volunteered, and to me that was the best wedding present we received, thanks guys.   Someday I will repay those favors in my own way.

After all this happened, I called my future wife to tell her we would have to pay the $300.00 for the building. She said "What? Forget it then, we'll just go rent another place". Then I reminded her that time was running out. I also told her about the trouble I just went through to get a duty watch together. So she reluctantly agreed to rent the building.

I went back to the ship's office and signed for the building.   It was a done deal.   The unit's kitchen was under renovations at the time, and I was wondering if it would be finished by February. The PO told me that it was touch and go. So with this news, I decided with my wife that we would just have a potluck dinner, and hopefully we would be able to use the kitchen's refrigerators at the very least.

The day before the wedding day, we were allowed to assemble a small crew to come in and decorate the building, after a previous party had left. I showed up in jeans and a T-shirt and welcomed my in-laws into the building. That was a nice moment for me. I talked a lot about my Navy career to them, and it was nice to have the one on one time with them as they toured the building.

Then it was time for the big day, everyone had worked so hard to help make this day happen for Kellie and me. We hired a DJ service, a Justice of the Peace, and rented a room across the parking lot at a nearby hotel. The only thing left to do was tie the knot.

I remember being one of the first to show up, along with my brother, future brother-in-law, and friend Rob. We all went into the Junior Ranks mess where I met with the duty watch crew. As a nice touch they were all dressed in their number 1 uniform. I asked the bartender if everything was ready. He could see I was visibly nervous. I couldn't stop pacing around so my brother told him to pour me a double scotch. The four of us had a quick shot and toasted my wedding day.

Having a shot with Jason, Darren & Rob

From there things just started happening, and the place started to fill up. My nervousness went away for a time while I played host to the many guests. Then things got formal again, and before I knew it those butterflies were back. The boys in uniform lined up at the side of the gym after everyone was seated. I could see them from where I stood at the entrance. Then it was time for me to come out. I'm not very good in front of crowds, and it was almost devastating to have everyone turn around in their seats to watch me walk down the aisle. When I reached the end and turned around, I raised my eyebrows at my brother-in-law and gave a big "Whew".

Signing the marriage certificate

Then came the wedding march, and the spotlight was off me. Everyone spun around in their chairs one more time to look at the door. Then, there she was, my whole life, my God she was so radiant that day. I will never forget the way she looked. During the vows, the JP tripped up a bit, but other than that things ran quite smoothly. Before I knew it, we were married.

We signed all the registers and what not, then we listened to a bunch of speeches. Then it was time to loosen the tie, cut loose and celebrate.

A short time after the wedding, my in-laws were over for a visit. My father in-law pulled out videotape that he had made of the wedding, and presented it to us. We all sat together and watched it for the first time.

The Receiving Line, Dad on the far left

That tape became even more of a keepsake for me later on. At the wedding, the wedding party and the parents all lined up in a receiving line. My father in-law gave his camera to a guest who in-turn, taped his own walk through the receiving line. At the end of the line was my dad, and the tape conveys the last images I have of my father speaking, smiling, and laughing. He died of cancer not much more than a year later.

WHEN WE WERE PIRATES

In the fall of 1995, I went to Victoria for a two week training exercise in small boats training. The exercise was designed to help us improve our tactics in intercepting vessels of interest, or stopping enemy ships from gaining access into our harbors.

I was all set to spend the next two weeks onboard a RHIB. Which is just a patrol boat that is open to the elements. But when I attended the opening lecture I found that I had lucked out and I would be spending the whole exercise onboard a YAG. As I described previously in this book, a YAG is equipped with two different sleeping quarters bellow decks as well as a kitchen and a bathroom.

We were supposed to be the bad guys, trying to slip past the patrollers at our own leisure. While our colleges had to patrol in the cold, day and night, we could just sit back and come at them whenever we felt like it. We designated ourselves as pirates and we didn't have to wear our uniforms. There was hardly any regular ship's routine to follow, except for keeping things clean. We didn't have a cook on board, but there was an engineer who volunteered and he did a great job. What a nice trip this was going to be.

Once or twice during those two weeks, we just didn't bother coming around for a whole day at a time. I remember playing a lot of card games below decks with the boys and just laughing away the whole trip. That was one of the easiest trips I had ever been on, I will always remember it. Sometimes you get on a crew, and you don't get enough chance to really get to know each other. That wasn't the case on this trip, there were a lot of times we spent laying in our racks talking to each other.

If we could pick and choose our trips, I would never say no to one like that. It was a good job while it lasted. Sometimes you get the hard jobs, but sometimes you get the occasional jobs like this. We all knew we were lucky, and I would say that crew had the best morale of any crew I had ever been a part of. I never heard anyone complain.

There was one night I remember when we decided to try to sneak into the harbor. It was pitch black outside when we dispatched our sea boat. We drove along very slowly until it was time to cut the engines to keep quite. We could see the patrol boats swirling around like sharks when we got out our paddles. We had all the time in the world to sneak in, so we quietly paddled along. We kept our voices low, as sound travels quite well on a quiet night like this.

As we paddled along, we moved in close to the shoreline. We thought the backdrop would provide camouflage. However, the patrol boats, paying particular attention to movement along the shoreline had spotted us. Or so it seemed. A strobe light from one of the boats shone right in our faces for the longest time. We all laid down in the boat right away. We were temporarily blinded. The light went away and then it came back, this happened a couple of times. We decided that we must not have been spotted, and as we nudged up against the land we carefully and slowly disembarked.

I was asked to stay behind with the boat as the other guys went to infiltrate headquarters. There was a big log on the shore that I lay down in front of. The boat rope wasn't long enough for me to lay behind the log. While I waited there, the strobe light searched the shore and ran across my body several times. I waited for what seemed like an eternity until the light finally just fixed on me. I heard the RHIB rev right up and start to come towards me. I kept lying down until I heard the loud hailer calling me. Then I stood up in the light and turned myself in.

I guess our mission was compromised when the land forces apprehended our guys when they tried to breach headquarters. I didn't know it at the time, but I was the last guy on the lam. Our boys confessed to my hideout, the RHIB was called to investigate, and I was immediately captured. Good work guys.

SRI TRIP ON THE GATES

In Late February of 1996, I left Edmonton for a weeklong trip aboard the Gate Vessel: HMCS Port De La Reine. A ship that I would later help decommission at the end of the year, but that's another story told previously in this book. The trip was intended for SRI's, which stands for Ship Readiness Inspections. SRI's are conducted by a team of specialists. This team is designed to assess a crew's operational readiness on a yearly basis, or whenever a significant change in crewmembers is made. These inspections deal with the crews' ability to come together as a fully functional team, as they are expected to run through a series of evolutions and safety drills one after the other. The crew must be able to achieve a solid state of oneness in order to pass the SRI's.

The drills are carried out at breakneck speed, so I was happy the trip only lasted one week, or so I thought. I was originally sent out with my home unit HMCS

Nonsuch, to help them pass their SRI's, although I hadn't planned on sailing avidly with that ship throughout the year. It was almost as though I was an augment to my own unit. Nearing the end of the week I was offered a two-week extension to do an extended series of SRI's for a crew that would represent the Western Region of Canada. I decided that since I was fresh from almost completing one week of SRI's, and I was making more money than I did back home at the time, I would help the Western Region crew. After those two weeks were up, I was asked by Calgary's unit to augment their crew's one-week inspection as well. I agreed, and by the end of it all, I was one very sea ready sailor. I had also finished off my OJT (on the job training) that paved the way for my promotion to Leading Seaman a month and a half later.

During these four weeks of SRI's, the part I remember the most was the two weeks I spent working for the Western Region. During those two weeks, I managed to be a big factor in the routine of the ship, and the things I did onboard affected the training schedule. During a man over board exercise, I happened to be the Life Buoy Sentry. A Life Buoy Sentry is a person who stands at the back of the boat to monitor the water in case a person falls overboard. If such a case arises, the Sentry will raise the alarm, throw out a Kisby ring, a smoke marker, and maintain visual contact with the MOB.

During the SRI's, the MOB is just a dummy with a life jacket on. Since it is a training scenario, they don't like you to throw the smoke marker. Apparently, it is quite expensive and must be replaced immediately. The SRI team wants to see you make an attempt to go for the smoke marker just to know that you are following all the right steps. But they will usually stop you and have you just thrown an empty milk jug filled with glow sticks. However, I remember the Captain saying at the beginning of the trip that if the SRI team fails to make you stop, then get that smoke marker off. Getting the smoke marker off looks good on the crew, and the Captain offered to buy a drink for whoever could do it.

Well guess what, I managed to fire off the smoke marker. I saw the MOB and I quickly looked around, I didn't see an SRI team member, and I couldn't believe nobody was stopping me. The dummy was dropped from a level above me. What I think happened was that one guy dropped the MOB, and another guy was going to jump out to monitor my reactions. They don't want to come out before the exercise starts because you will be expecting something. However, I just had a feeling that a MOBex was going to be the next thing so I was on high alert. I think I spotted the damn thing before it even hit the water, and I immediately launched the smoke marker.

Thick orange smoke billowed out of the marker. The smoke is good for an hour I guess. We had to launch the sea boat to recover it, but the guys were having a hell of a time trying to submerge the thing to stop it from smoking. These markers are designed to be able to float through big waves, and in rough seas without dousing out the smoke. After spending almost an hour recovering the marker, it looked as though we were going to have to work harder to complete our schedule. But once again, I would throw a crimp into those plans.

Another sailor came by to relieve me from Life Buoy Sentry after the exercise was over. I was on my way to another post when an SRI member approached me and told me to go down a hatch and lie down at the bottom of it pretending to be injured. So I went down the hatch, but I didn't just lie at the bottom of it, instead I wrapped and twisted my legs through the rungs at the bottom of the ladder. When I didn't arrive at my next post they sent a search party to look for me. When they discovered me, they yelled down at me for a reaction. I didn't answer, instead of just pretending to be hurt, I pretended I was passed out. This went beyond the purpose of the exercise. The SRI team conducted this exercise to assess the response time to finding a missing crewmember. However, they decided to let the exercise carry on because my crew seemed so intent on helping me. They had a hell of a time untangling my legs from the ladder, and I wasn't offering any help. Then they struggled to put me into a stretcher to carry me up the ladder.

At the top of the ladder, they tried to assess my responsiveness, but I remained quiet. Somebody opened one of my eyes, and I tried to make only the whites of it show. I heard somebody laugh, and I tried my hardest not to. The crew went as far as calling a helicopter to fly out and rescue me before a fuming SRI team leader finally had enough and stopped the exercise.

In the end, we had no time left in the day for the rest of our exercises. A lot of guys came up to me later to thank me because they didn't want to have to do the other exercises, but I wasn't too popular with the SRI team.

PROMOTION AT SEA

In March of 1996, while I was sailing aboard the vessel, the HMCS Porte De La Reine, I completed my on the job work experience package. In doing so, I set myself up with the opportunity for promotion to Leading Seaman later that year. This trip was my longest stay onboard a gate vessel, and hence my most productive. I have told a few different stories from that voyage, three of which are part of this book.

I received my on the job training package after completing my first trades course in the fall of 1994. The following year, when I did my longest overall stint on a ship, the HMCS Kootenay, I signed off three-quarters of that package. After that tour, I took some time off from serving at sea. Instead I engaged in local training, as well as working on the coast at the small boat section. Unfortunately none of these activities were part of my package.

But in 1996, I heard of a trip on the De La Reine that was to conduct SRI training and work ups. This means that the ship was going to be practicing all kinds of evolutions. To me that meant the possibility of signing off my package. I eagerly signed up for the trip hoping to achieve my second promotion in the Reserves.

The trip was long and hard and punishing. No sooner had we started the work up phase of the training than we were gearing up for our first evolution. When we finished the first scenario, I remember thinking OK it's break time. I started to head down towards the cafeteria when a Master Seaman asked, "Where are you going?". It was time to set up the rigging for the next evolution. He handed me a schedule of the ship's events. When I looked at it I thought, "This is unreal." The evolutions were jam packed one after another, after another, and so on.

Except for basic training, this was the hardest tour I have ever served on with the Reserves. However, the days went by fairly quickly seeing as the work kept coming at us. Every time you thought there was a chance to sit down for a rest it was time to do something else. It was just relentless.

By the end of that trip, I think I was the most seaworthy I have ever been in my entire career. I was able to have my package completely signed off, and I was eager to be promoted. Being on that ship as an Able Seaman, I saw how we had to work a little harder than some of the senior Leading Seaman onboard. Some of the Leading Seaman would be in charge of the men during the evolutions, but there were some Junior Leading Seaman who helped out on the lines and such. All I know is that I wanted my promotion as soon as possible. My days of being an Able Seaman and getting ordered around so much were about to be a thing of the past.

I remember taking my package into the cafeteria at lunchtime and telling the other Able Seaman that I wasn't going to be one of them for too much longer. And after lunch, I eagerly approached one of the officers onboard and said, "Here's my package". I thought he could take it and just promote me right away, at least that's what I was telling everyone in the cafeteria. He told me that I would have to bring the package back home with me to my home unit and they would look at it and then send it off to headquarters. It was going to take a couple of months before I would be promoted. After that, all I could do was bitch and moan about my promotion.

One day shortly after we left port the Captain called the crew to attention on the well deck. An ex sailor was invited onto the ship and he had with him a big bottle of rum and an urn. In the urn were the ashes of someone he knew, and that person had requested a burial at sea. In an old Navy tradition gone by, we were all given a tot of rum to drink as the ceremony was conducted. It was a solemn moment and it made me forget about my own worries. But before we were dismissed my name was called and I was supposed to step forward in front of the Captain. I thought I was going to get in trouble for all the complaining I had been doing.

Instead, I received an impromptu promotion to the fictitious rank of Acting Leading Seaman. The Captain and the First Officer took off my Able Seaman epaulets and put on Leading Seaman epaulets in their place. Except these new epaulets had an A for "Acting" written just above the two chevrons in yellow grease pencil. I was allowed to wear that rank for the rest of my duration onboard. And when I was sent back into the ranks the boys all ribbed me a little bit, but they congratulated me as well.

ONE BIG FISH

During my time aboard the HMCS Kootenay, I saw a lot of places and experienced a lot of different things. That contract remains to this day, the longest one I have been on during my entire career with the Reserves. It was also the biggest warship I sailed on, and it had the largest crew size I ever served with. The possessions I have of that ship are very dear to me, as the Kootenay is no longer in service. In my home, there is a hand painted ship's crest mounted on a wood plaque hanging above my bar. Every time I look at it, I remember those days.

This ship also held one more record for my career. A record that is a little more obscure than all the rest. It happened on a day while we were at anchor surrounded by a horseshoe of beautifully treed and mountainous landscape. I was standing watch as the life buoy sentry at the back of the boat, and there were quite a few sailors bustling around behind me.

Amidst the activity, there was one lone sailor fishing over the side of the ship. He wasn't in anyone's way, and he was hardly attracting any attention. Although every time I looked over at him, he seemed to be acting as though there was something on the end of his line. People asked him every now and then if he had something, and he never seemed to give a straight answer. He just kept giving illusive answers like, "I'm not sure". He was acting pretty nonchalant about the whole thing. Maybe he just wanted to land the damn thing before he talked about it too much. I figure he just didn't want to jinx things. By and by, people would talk to him for a bit and then leave him alone without drawing too much attention.

Where the fish was caught

After a couple of hours, this man was starting to appear quite visibly exhausted, and by now the crowd had started to form and the attention was undeniable. It didn't take too long after the crowd had started to form that the news spread throughout the ship. By now, I was off watch and I joined the eager crowd.

Just when it seemed like this guy had had enough, the order was given to launch the sea boat. One of the two Petty Officers who was in charge of my department got into the boat, pistol in hand. Those who were standing close to the edge were able to look over the side to watch the action. I wasn't so fortunate. But as I stood there waiting I heard the pistol fire three times, along with the sound of the bullets hitting the side of our ship.

After a few moments of nothing happening, the people who could see over the edge started to cheer. Then one of them signaled for the crane operator to hoist the sea boat back onboard. When the boat was recovered, it was there for all to see. The sailor had caught a massive Halibut, just under four feet long, and I can't remember how much they said it weighed. It took two guys to hold up the fish for pictures, and you could see the blood running down it from the perfect little bullet holes in it's head. It looked like something out of a hunting magazine, and it was the largest fish I ever saw anyone catch.

For the next couple of days, that Halibut was one of the choices on the menu in various dishes. I never tried it though. One of the things I'm often teased about is that I'm a sailor who doesn't like seafood. Go figure.

DRIVING THE HURRICANE

In November of 1996, I was sent to Stanley Park in Vancouver to participate in a tactical boat training exercise. I was originally sent out to participate as part of a RHIB crew, to defend the harbour against incoming enemy vessels that were to be simulated by using boats called Hurricanes. It was going to be our job to intercept these boats and do a proper investigation of the crew onboard. The Hurricanes are slightly smaller and less powerful than the RHIBs are. But they were to be driven by our more skilled and senior drivers, to give the RHIB drivers the best training possible.

In order to drive the RHIBs, you require a training course to receive your ticket. Since I don't have my RHIB ticket, I was just there to be part of the crew and help with hailing vessels, line handling, navigation, communication, and any other duties I could perform.

When we arrived, we were told we would be camping in Stanley Park, and the first night we were assigned to our tents. I remember the Master Seaman, who I traveled with from Nonsuch, being so intent on finding us a good working heater for our tent before he tended to making his own cot and getting his sleeping bag ready. He made sure the tent was properly closed at all times, and he was the last guy to get his personal kit squared away. He was a good guy, and he tried to look after his crew the best he could. He didn't always get along with his superiors but that was OK, he got along well with his subordinates. He didn't care to rub elbows with those in charge, he was in our corner, and that's why he was well liked. The kind of guy you could lean on, in fact he volunteered as bartender at my wedding.

Even though we got the best heater the Master Seaman could find, it was still pretty damn cold. I couldn't fall asleep even though I was dead tired. I was starting to get that sick feeling you get when you desperately need sleep, but it's hard to fall asleep when you're shivering. I didn't know what we were in for in the morning, but just getting through the night was going to be a relief. Tomorrow morning, we would probably be inside the Gym getting a lecture on the day's events, I couldn't wait.

However, I needed to get some sleep, so I looked over at the Master Seaman to see what his trick was. I saw that he was wearing his floater suit. The floater suit is a full body suit that we wear out on the water. It's like a snowsuit but much more expensive and it has the capability of being buoyant. He looked like someone who had just come of watch and passed out from exhaustion, but at least he was asleep. I decided to put mine on as well, so I hopped out of bed to get it from my bag. For a brief few moments things went from bad to worse when I first got out of my sleeping bag. But once I put on my floater suit I went out like a light.

By morning the temperature had dropped a few degrees and my shivering woke me up. I felt wet, I guess the warmth of the floater suit had caused me to sweat during the night. What a way to wake up. After brushing my teeth out the back door of the tent, I went to breakfast. Breakfast was served in another tent with the flaps pulled wide open. There were a few picnic tables inside, and they were wet with the morning dew. Breakfast consisted of dropping your foil bag of food into a boiling pot of water on a portable camp stove. Most people tried to huddle around the stove for warmth.

After breakfast, it was finally time to go inside to be tasked off to our boats and to go over a few patrol procedures. For the first time in quite a few hours, I warmed up. After the meeting let out, the weather outside had improved some. You could still see your breath, but by now the sun was out and you could feel its warmth. I was ready to face the day.

We all went down to the boats to conduct pre sail checks on them before flashing them up. Once we got down there, it turned out that the Hurricane crews would be one driver short. One of the drivers, a local guy, called in sick that morning. And I guess that since I was one of the only Leading Seaman who wasn't driving a RHIB, they asked me to drive the Hurricane. I didn't even have a small boat operator's ticket, and at the time, I hadn't been a Leading Seaman for very long. To make matters worse, they gave me a crew made up of all the non-essential junior bodies, one Able Seaman, and two Ordinary Seaman.

I wasn't exactly sure what to look for during the pre sail checks, so I tried to keep my back to the Petty Officer who was watching me. I'm not a navigator, or a radio communicator, so I was hoping my two Ordinary Seaman knew something, good grief. I figured the one Able Seaman I had for a bowsman might have some seamanship skills. But if he didn't that was OK, he was the same trade as me and I knew what to do as far as my own job. I was a little nervous to get underway, but I could tell my crew looked up to me for leadership because I had the two chevrons on my shoulder.

I think I had my crew convinced that I knew what I was doing, so we decided we were ready to get underway. Once we left the jetty area, I told my communicator to radio in and do a radio check. And between her and the navigator, it became apparent that we had a bit of a problem. I stopped the boat and let it idle in the water. Then I told my Able Seaman to get behind the wheel while I had a smoke. He looked a little surprised, but he seemed eager enough. I let him drive for quite some time while I helped the girls figure things out. Headquarters knew that we had a few bugs to get out, so they sort of helped us along the way.

We made quick progression, and as the day went on we were performing quite well as a viable crew. I let everyone take turns driving until nightfall. For safety reasons we had to keep everyone in their best positions when the darkness came, so I drove the Hurricane. But that didn't mean we couldn't still have a little bit of fun. With the poor visibility I thought it would be fun to open the throttle right up for a moment or two, so I did. My crew was a little surprised, but I could tell by their faces, they were having a good time. Suddenly, the boat became airborne and everyone's expression went from excited to scared shitless. I guess we must have hit a rouge wave, we sure didn't see it in the dark. Once we landed I put the throttle into neutral right away, and another wave crashed over us and soaked us all. After that, all was calm, and within a couple of seconds we all had a good laugh.

At the end of the year it was stated in my personal evaluation that I was a valuable team member that weekend. That I didn't complain about the cold weather which was effecting morale, and that I learned the systems of the Hurricane independently, and in such a short time.

WORKING ON THE CANNON

At the end of the training year in 2001, my department was asked if anyone would like to come in during the summer to work on the gun. The gun was this great big deck mounted cannon-like contraption that was donated to our unit a few years ago from who knows where. It sits in the corner of the parking lot adjacent to Kingsway Avenue in Edmonton. I guess it belonged to an old US warship in the 40's. The barrel of this gun is about fifteen feet long, and I think the inside diameter is about 3 inches or so, but I could be wrong. It has a big deck at the back of it and there are two fixed chairs on either side for the operators.

The gun has been there for a few years now, and has previously been the sight of controversy. I remember the news catching my attention one night when I heard that a bomb disposal unit was doing an investigation down at Nonsuch. Apparently someone had been seen placing a suspicious package underneath the gun. It later turned out to be a harmless package, I guess it was just somebody's idea of a joke. I was told that on another occasion, resident businesses in the area were complaining that they didn't want the damn thing pointed at them, which makes sense. So there it sits in our parking lot, pointed straight at our building.

Anyway, there were five of us that ended up working on this thing, but never more than four at any given time. Most of the time I was in charge of the work, except when the Master Seaman felt like showing up to help. It was our job to give this gun a fresh coat of "Ship's side grey," paint. And they told us that we had only the month of June to work on it. I guess the Admiral was supposed to come visit our unit that August. And the work we were doing was just a small part of the overall work happening at the unit to spruce it up for his visit.

We were given Monday and Wednesday nights to work on it for three hours a night, and there was an optional full day Saturday, which consisted of six hours. That was also the day we got the least done since we were the only ones at the unit on Saturdays. There were commercial painters working during the day painting the main building, so we just used their supplies at night. The first night I looked at the gun I thought, we could do this on time no problem. There was a lot of paint peeling off it, so the first thing we decided to do was to get out the buffing wheels and remove all the loose paint chips. For the first couple of nights this was all we did, and we worked exclusively on the lower half of the gun. Then came time to start buffing off the upper areas on the gun so we could keep up to the schedule.

That's when it happened, while buffing off the upper portions of the gun, we found that a lot of the metal was made of solid brass. Around the compasses, along the cranks, on the two front guards, and encasing the huge oil compartment, there was nothing but beautiful solid brass. I guess in those days brass was probably easier to mold with the technology they had back then. I can understand the whole thing being painted grey back in the days when this thing was attached to a warship. But we all thought this gun would make one hell of an impressive display if we exposed all the brass accents and polished them up.

We were starting to spend a lot of time on removing the decades of paint from the brass parts. We even got out some tools and dismantled what we could so we could work on them in the shop. Nearing the end of our allotted working time, a Petty Officer came wandering out from the building to check on our progress. I was sure that when he saw the brass showing, he would give us an extension. But all he saw was that we hadn't done any painting yet, and he told us to just paint over everything. I'm not sure that he appreciated the value of brass.

I argued with him for a while, and he told me that he would get confirmation from a higher authority. When he came back he again gave the order to paint everything. I painted everything that wasn't brass and then I withdrew my name from the project. I just couldn't bring myself to paint over the brass. When I came back for training the next year, I saw that somebody else had completed the job.

I do look back on that project fondly however. Having a portable radio blaring away while we worked, horsing around in the shop during breaks, and having a few beer together after work. There were also a few funny moments of dealing with the public when we worked. One guy asked us if the old relic still worked, well at least we waited until he was gone to have a good laugh at that one.

FOOSBALL NIGHTS

During the course of my career, a favorite pastime of mine was playing foosball. We had an old table at my home unit that was donated by a Master Seaman at some point in the early days of my career. I remember my first couple of games on that table. I was absolutely slaughtered by the Master Seaman. At first I thought this wasn't the game for me, and I didn't really play it for the next couple of years.

Eventually that Master Seaman left Nonsuch, and I took a renewed interest in the game. I played quite avidly for the rest of my career. By 1994 and for the next couple of years the competition was pretty heady, but by 1996 I started to break away from the rest. There was a solid circle of players at the time, but when one of them was promoted out of the mess, and with my skills ever progressing, that circle died off.

I was the only one who kept playing, always hovering around the table at break times, and playing whoever would play me. Then, around 1998 a new circle of dedicated players started forming. This new group became very solid by 1999. There were four of us who played all the time no matter what, but there was a larger circle of at least 10 or more quality players. It all depended on who was away, or on contract at the time.

I was still the guy to beat, but the league stayed strong and flourished on into the next millennium. Mostly we played doubles, this way we could make the games closer depending on who we matched up. This was something that I hadn't thought of the first time around, which eventually made the league fold. This second time around, I was smarter. Playing doubles helped maintain interest amongst the players, and placing small wagers on the games, like making the losers buy the winners beer, made for quite a bit of excitement.

In the early 2000's, I lived for the game. It got so that the only thing I thought about when it was time for a training night was how much foosball I was going to get in. Often times I caught shit from my wife for coming home an hour late. The game got that addicting for everyone, and at peak times in the season when the players were at their best, we were really something to watch. There were many times when our games started to attract crowds, and a lot of the time people were leaving the mess late after break time because of it. The message must have come down dozens of times that there was to be no foosball playing during anytime in the working schedule. We would try to adhere to this, but often times we would start sliding and have to be reminded again.

I don't know if our superiors realized it or not, but I think that foosball game was responsible for at least 5 solid years of good attendance and moral amongst a lot of sailors in the Junior Ranks mess. If they had decided to take that table away it would have been devastating, but there was definitely a power struggle over it.

Being one of the four core players, I can remember how we always talked about trying to set up some sort of tournament with prize money. We discussed how some of the proceeds would go to charity, but at the time of writing this book that still never happened. And we always fantasized about being professional foosball players, if there was even such a thing.

I think that foosball eventually started to lead to the demise of my career, because I didn't want to be promoted out of the junior ranks mess. I didn't want to leave those good times behind, and so my career wasn't progressing as fast as the Navy wanted it to.

After having played the game constantly and for many years, I would love the chance to play that Master Seaman who beat me all those years ago. I could probably beat him now with one hand tied behind my back.

BOARDING AN OVERSEAS VESSEL

In March of 1996, while completing a tour as an augment for Calgary's unit, we were called in to investigate a vessel from overseas. Our ship was at anchor in an inlet just off the coast of Victoria, and we were enjoying a barbecue celebrating a successful day of SRI inspections when we got the call.

At the time I had already started into my second beer, and I had just powered down a steak, so I was a little unsure about going. Also the overseas ship was much larger than ours was. Our ship was almost completely crewed by Reserve sailors, so it was a surprise that we were even asked to inspect their ship. However, the Captain was told that if he wasn't comfortable with boarding them, that we could just observe them and wait for a destroyer to come along and do the job.

Instead our Captain sent the message down to his officers, which then it made it's way to us, that he intended for our crew to form a boarding party. So we were called to attention on the well deck, and volunteers were asked to step forward. There were enough eager volunteers that the boarding party crew was established without a hassle. There were a few men, and a couple of officers on the crew. And a good buddy of mine from basic training was there to drive the sea boat.

The sailor's were given a quick briefing before being sent on their way. I did lend a hand to the mission as far as helping to dispatch the sea boat. I wished my old friend good luck with a pat on the back. Then it was back to my beer, and waiting for the safe return of my fellow sailors.

Off they went bouncing along in the sea boat towards the ship that dwarfed ours. I watched as my buddy parked the boat by a ladder on the overseas vessel. The boarding crew climbed the ladder, and began investigating the ship. My buddy stayed with the rescue boat at the bottom of the ladder. Our fellow sailors were investigating the ship for quite some time, but I guess we never got a distress call from them. Actually, of the crew that stayed behind, unless you were an officer, you really didn't know what was going on over there.

I periodically looked over to my buddy in the rescue boat; he never seemed to look worried, so I took that to mean that everything was going OK. Although you still had to worry about your colleges until they came back safely.

Once they all did return safely, we exuberantly pulled them back onboard and began to bombard them with questions. I handed my buddy a cold beer and shook his hand. Apparently the sea boat received a slight puncture in it from the ladder on the overseas vessel. My buddy made the gutsy decision that it wasn't significant enough to end the mission and he monitored it the whole time, although the boat seemed a little floppy to me when it returned. As I talked with him, a couple of our Ordinary Seaman repaired the hole.

Soon we got back down to the business of enjoying our barbecue as the boarding party told us of their experience. I guess they didn't find anything onboard that ship that was contraband, however they did notice a lot of cartons of cigarettes taped to the underside of tables and chairs. I guess they had a little more duty free items than they were entitled to or something like that. Also, our boys said they had to watch a few videotapes they found onboard to ensure there was no illegal footage on them either.

All in the entire mission was a success, and the reason it seemed to take so long, I was told, was to allow for adequate diplomacy between them and us. In the end, we got a call from headquarters commending us on a job well done, and our Captain toasted the whole ship's company.

About 5½ years later, while doing a training weekend in Victoria near the end of 2001, I met up with a sailor who was part of that boarding party. I asked him again about what happened onboard that ship, and he basically told me more or less, the same information I already knew. But he also told me that it was quite the rush to board the vessel, and that I should have joined the crew. I smiled at him and said, "Maybe the next one".

SOFTBALL WITH THE BOYS

At the end of the training year, as a yearly tradition, our unit usually has a wrap up barbecue as well as a sports day involving the whole ship's company. And it was no different at the end of the training year in 1997. This year, during the sports part of the day, we divided the sailors into two teams and played a spirited afternoon of softball.

Prior to that softball game, I had played hardball in my local community circuit for the previous 14 seasons. I knew some of the members of Nonsuch had put a softball team together in the past, but I had always refused to play due to my commitments to community baseball. But at the end of the 1996 season, after being rejected by a major league talent scout, I quit baseball.

At the end of our sports day, I was asked once again to play for the Nonsuch softball team over the summer. With baseball being a part of my life for almost as long as I could remember, I just couldn't say no. In the last few years of my ball career, the competition was getting fiercer, and the fun of the game had started to diminish. But I was about to rediscover that fun and have my love for the sport rekindled.

I showed up for the first game, wearing my baseball pants with a long black T-shirt, wristbands, and batting gloves. And when I looked around at all the other players, I looked like I was a professional ringer. Some of the players on our team who had played together in previous years, had matching T-shirts with Nonsuch written on them.

The players told me when I arrived for the first game, that the team we were playing against was our rival team and that they had beaten Nonsuch in last year's playoffs. Apparently they were always a tough team to beat, as they perennially dominated the league. I hoped that this year I could make the difference. Well, we ended our first game in a tie, and I was a big factor in that end result.

We were the home team, so we had last bats. It was the top of the last inning, and they were up by a score of 5 to 2. The bases were loaded, there were two outs, and I was playing first base. Then it happened, the batter turned on a pitch and smoked a line drive very low to the ground, about half way between first and second base. It was definitely a base hit in any league. I've even seen line shots like that end up as base hits in the major leagues. They would have easily scored a couple more runs, and we never would have managed to tie the game like we did in the bottom half of the inning.

In all my years of competitive baseball, I had made the best play of my life that day on the softball field. It's funny how life works sometimes. This was one of those plays where you surprise even yourself, and I wasn't exactly sure how I did it. At the crack of the bat, I didn't think about it, I just reacted. It was just a reflex, and it was as though it wasn't even me doing it. To make the catch I made, I reacted to the play at the moment the ball hit the bat. I'm not even sure I could see the direction the ball was going but I just started running. I ran all out towards second base, and then I just dove. At the bitter end of my reach, I felt the ball go into my glove. When I hit the ground I slid pretty far due to my own momentum, and I was lucky not to drop the ball in that violent landing.

When I stood up, I acted like I just made a routine catch as I flipped the ball towards the mound, and I turned to walk off the field. My teammates however, mobbed me as though we had just won the World Series. Even the other team applauded my efforts, and I could hear onlookers talking about the catch, what a moment. We were fired up as we went into the home half of the last inning. We managed to tie the game, and I had a chance to be the hero again. It was my turn to bat with two outs and the bases loaded. Unfortunately I was swinging for the fences, and I ended up flying out. My team was happy enough with our start to the season though, because this was a team they usually lost against. I guess this year we sent them a message.

The end of the season came, and we were pitted against these guys for the playoffs. It was supposed to be a best of 3 game series. We shocked them by winning the first game and we needed one more win to become champions. But sadly, our team fell apart and we lost the next two games. But I had an absolute blast that year; it was great to love the game again.

There was a buddy of mine on that team, and throughout the season we kept in competition against each other for home runs. At the end of the season we each had six, which was a tie for the most on our team. We both ended up playing one more year with Nonsuch. After that, he quit the Reserves, and I was just starting a family of my own. Maybe one day my son will take up the game, and I will once again enjoy the sport vicariously through him.

Printed in the United States
by Baker & Taylor Publisher Services